The Best Canadian Poetry in English 2010

The Best Canadian Poetry

in English
2010

Edited by
Lorna Crozier

Series Editor
Molly Peacock

Tightrope Books

Tightrope Books
602 Markham Street
Toronto, Ontario
Canada M6G 2L8
www.TightropeBooks.com

ONTARIO ARTS COUNCIL
CONSEIL DES ARTS DE L'ONTARIO

EDITOR: Lorna Crozier
SERIES EDITOR: Molly Peacock
MANAGING EDITOR: Heather Wood
COPY EDITOR: Alanna Lipson
COVER DESIGN: Karen Correia Da Silva
COVER ART: Viktor Mitic
TYPESETTING: Shirarose Wilensky

Canada Council
for the Arts

Conseil des Arts
du Canada

Produced with the support of the Canada Council for the Arts and the Ontario Arts Council.

Printed in Canada.

LIBRARY AND ARCHIVES CANADA CATALOGUING IN PUBLICATION

The best Canadian poetry in English, 2010 / editor: Lorna Crozier.

ISBN 978-1-926639-16-1

1. Canadian poetry (English)–21st century. i. Crozier, Lorna

PS8293.1.B48 2009   C811'.608   C2009-903917-6

CONTENTS

Molly Peacock	vii	Prologue
Lorna Crozier	xi	Introduction
Ken Babstock	3	Lee Atwater in Blowing Snow
John Barton	5	Mill Creek Reverdie
Anne Compton	7	Heat in April
Allan Cooper	8	Two Glimpses
Mary Dalton	9	Three Centos
Barry Dempster	13	Mary Lake Writing Retreat
Kildare Dobbs	15	It
Don Domanski	16	Gloria Mundi
Glen Downie	18	Nocturnal Visitors
Sue Goyette	19	This Last Lamp
Rosemary Griebel	21	Wonder
Adrienne Gruber	22	The Rope
Jamella Hagen	24	Driving Daytona
Steven Heighton	25	Some Other Just Ones
Warren Heiti	27	The Day
M.G.R. Hickman-Barr	29	Cattle Egret
Maureen Hynes	31	The Last Cigarette
Michael Johnson	33	In Praise of the Village Idiot
Jim Johnstone	35	Disgraceland
Sonnet L'Abbé	36	The Trees Have Loved Us All Along
Fiona Tinwei Lam	37	Aquarium
Evelyn Lau	38	Swimming Lessons
Katherine Lawrence	40	Dear—
Ross Leckie	43	The Critique of Pure Reason
Tim Lilburn	45	Rupert's Land
Dave Margoshes	50	The Chicken Coop
Jim Nason	51	Black Ice
Catherine Owen	52	White Sale
P.K. Page	53	Cullen in Old Age
Rebecca Leah Păpucaru	57	Rosalind Franklin in Open-Toe Sandals

Contents

Marilyn Gear Pilling	59	Billy Collins Interviewed On Stage at Chautauqua
Lenore & Beth Rowntree	63	7 lbs. 6 oz.
Armand Garnet Ruffo	67	The Tap is Dripping Memory
Lori Saint-Martin	69	Quatre fruits/Four Fruits
Peter Sanger	74	Sea Horse (for M.)
Robyn Sarah	76	Messenger
Eleonore Schönmaier	78	Weightless
David Seymour	79	The Photo Double
Melanie Siebert	81	Ditch
Sue Sinclair	82	Cherry Trees
Karen Solie	83	Postscript
Nick Thran	86	Aria with a Mirror and No Earplugs
Carey Toane	87	Seventy-two-hour emergency
Anne-Marie Turza	89	Anthem for a Small Country
Paul Tyler	90	Manitoba Maples
Patrick Warner	92	The Mole
Zachariah Wells	93	To the Superb Lyrebird, that Cover Band of the Australian Bush
Patricia Young	94	Night-Running
David Zieroth	97	How Brave
Jan Zwicky	99	Autobiography
	101	Poem Notes & Commentaries
	125	Poet Biographies
	139	Longlist of 50 Poems
	143	Magazines Considered for the 2010 Edition
	149	Permission Acknowledgements
	157	Editor Biographies

PROLOGUE

Poetry is the art that responds to the anxiety of living . . .

Welcome to *The Best Canadian Poetry in English 2010*. Each year, as we take the pulse of the nation by searching for the best poems published in our literary journals in the previous year, we unearth just what's engaging and bothering Canadians. Though we never set out to select poetry with particular styles or subjects, we find that we can trust our poets to nose out important ideas in our cultural conversation. This year poets writing in English are circling, sniffing, and nudging issues dealing with our environment. They are engaging with our seasons, our weather, our critters, our blossoms, our trees, mountains, river valleys, and skies, and doing so with their whole spirits and language. Or should I say with their whole animal natures?

Nobody can write a straight, old-fashioned nature poem these days. Reverence for the natural world, once the pure contact that defined the soul, is now fraught with ethical issues. You can barely look at a tree without imagining clear cutting, spy a deer without being seized by the thought of its shrinking habitat, or certainly glimpse a photo of a polar bear without a spasm of imagining its extinction. The damaged earth provokes a helplessness that can make a person want to turn her back on it all, sinking into a sealed-off air-conditioned room lit only by the glow of a computer screen.

Or it can provoke poetry. Poetry is the art that responds to the anxiety of living. And here are fifty poems (plus a longlist of the titles of fifty more) that brilliantly attempt to make sense of the contradictions of living in the twenty-first century. Although most

of us suffer the inconsistencies of, say, assiduously sorting our re-
cyclable garbage one minute and painting a bookcase with a toxic
spray can the next, poets thrive on incongruity. Paradox is the
poet's art. To take hold of an image and invert it is the basis of
both disorientation *and* metaphor. These poems take the emo-
tional states of our lives and turn them inside out, examining their
oppositions and finding, usually through refusing to resolve such
conflicts, a way for the readers of poetry to examine and live with
them.

The remarkable poems in this collection were chosen by our
guest editor for 2010, Lorna Crozier. She valiantly read more than
150 issues of 45 magazines, published both in print and online.
The complete list of magazines, including their contact infor-
mation, can be found at the end of this book. We feature it to
demonstrate the wide variety and locations of our sources, and
the liveliness of the national literary scene. Not only did Crozier
shoulder this work, but she also managed our collaboration of
the final selection with characteristic good humour and *joie de
vivre*. It took some heart-wrenching decisions to narrow the list
down, since many poems being published in Canadian journals
(from the well-known magazines such as *The Malahat Review* or
The Fiddlehead to newer, less well-known journals such as *Riddle
Fence*) more than met our criteria of displaying both passion and
virtuosity. We are very proud to include the longlist of fifty poems
to give our readers an idea of the breadth and range of excellence
in poetry this year.

Each of our guest editors has had such an individual feel for
poetry in their particular year that our annual anthologies have

presented vastly different pools of poets. We are delighted to be able to introduce poets unfamiliar to our readers with each volume, and to introduce various forms of poetry as well. This year we include prose poems, the hybrid form that pushes the definition of poetry to its essentials without its lines, and formal poetry that uses those very lines with regular music and rhyme.

Since our inaugural edition two years ago, *The Best Canadian Poetry in English* has become the standard anthology for all who are curious about Canadian poetry but need a place for such curiosity to begin. Our anthologies are now in living rooms, waiting rooms, university and high school classrooms, and no doubt bathrooms, too. Perhaps what's pleased us most is that our 2009 volume has appeared on the *Globe and Mail* poetry bestsellers list. This is the collection that represents Canada abroad; when poetry readers throughout the world seek to know about Canadian poetry, this is the volume they grab from the shelf. Regularly we launch *The Best Canadian* series in cities throughout the country. This year we will be launching in Vancouver, Victoria, Toronto, and Montreal, as well as in New York City.

Many individuals put hours of hard work into this volume, and foremost is Halli Villegas, the visionary who began Tightrope Books and whose energy makes it thrive. Editors Heather Wood and Shirarose Wilensky tirelessly handle the massive number of details and decisions that help complete each anthology. The poets in our 2008 and 2009 editions deserve another round of thanks and applause for all the readings across the country they have organized and participated in, and both inaugural guest editor Stephanie Bolster and last year's guest editor A. F. Moritz have our continued

Prologue

gratitude for the support they have given to our series. We thank David Bigham and Michael Groden for their contributions to our efforts, as well as designer Karen Correia Da Silva for the engaging look of our book.

Recently at the West Chester Poetry Conference in the United States, our anthology was discussed on a panel, and I made a distinction between Canadian and American poets in terms of their contracts with their readers. While the American poet often feels that she or he must impress with fireworks in the first few lines, feeling some desperation to hold a reader, I do not sense this pressure in Canadian poets. They have a different relationship with the reader, and I think it is one of trust. A Canadian poet feels that to start slow and gather the individual strangeness of perception is possible because that Canadian poet can trust the reader to wait to find out what will happen in the poem. The reader of Canadian poetry does not say, *Impress me.* Instead, this reader says, *Engage me.* With spunk, with vivacity, with terror, with humour, and with love, these fifty poets certainly do.

Molly Peacock
TORONTO

INTRODUCTION

Holding Feathers in Your Teeth

Naming takes place almost immediately after creation in the Book of Genesis. God, who perhaps understood the difficulty of the task, washed his hands of it and gave the responsibility to the man he'd just moulded from clay and spittle. There are two different kinds of Adams, according to Don McKay in one of his talks about poetry. The one who is the scientist, Don says, observes the animals, names them, and goes home happy to a warm supper and a good sleep, his job complete. The Adam who is the poet observes them, names them, goes home, and can't eat or sleep. He knows he didn't get it right and has to try again. And again.

Eve had yet to enter the picture. Who knows what she would have come up with had she been standing by Adam's wounded side as the animals paraded by and as his attention turned to the flora of the garden? Perhaps like Sonnet L'Abbé, she'd have eschewed a single noun like *tree*. Instead, she'd have rhapsodized about a tree's marvellous cognition and sensory acuity, its ability to sense her smell, to feel her heat. How can a single noun come close to what L'Abbé's poem, "The Trees Have Loved Us All Along," reveals about this sensate gigantic presence we take for granted on the street corner?

Word by word a poem is built. The choice of one over another implies an attitude and reflects the writer's beliefs, insights, and character. Think of forestry bosses calling the killing of trees "harvesting," or of Dick Cheney calling water boarding "robust interrogation." Albert Camus went so far as to say, "Naming an object inaccurately means adding to the unhappiness of the world." Well, no poet wants to do that! And yet, is it possible to name anything accurately? Do words exist to describe the loss of love, a porcupine, the sadness around an aging parent? Even the simplest of things resist our craft and sullen art. Carey Toane's "Seventy-two-hour emergency" asserts, "There is no other word for Ziploc."

Steven Heighton's poem in this anthology collates an assortment of people whom he deems worthy of praise. Among them are the ones "Who redeem from neglect a gorgeous, long-orphaned word." His pithy character sketches conclude with the line, "These people, without knowing it, are saving the world." In the poem following Heighton's, Warren Heiti becomes one of these saviours by redeeming the rare words *alethic* and *palinodic*, both adjectives he uses to describe different kinds of light. Peter Sanger, at the beginning of his "Sea Horse," Ogden-Nash-like distinguishes *hippocampus* from *hippopotamus,* two multi-syllabic nouns that sound alike but differ vastly in what they signify. Though these Linnaean designations usually shy away from poetry, Sanger puts them to delightful use.

Struggling with language every time they do what they do best, poets understand its inadequacies better than anyone else, and they've understood this flaw at the heart of words since pen was first put to paper. More than four hundred years ago, Shakespeare's *King Lear* masterfully alerted the audience to the slippery slope of language. Not the King but the fool, with his paradoxes and word plays, speaks the most wisely and truthfully. And King Lear, the biggest fool of all, believes the false praise of daughters Goneril and Regan, missing the modesty and honesty of Cordelia's lament: "my love's / more richer than my tongue."

Lorna Crozier

Ken Babstock records his own linguistic limitations in "Lee Atwater in Blowing Snow." After a stunning opening, "Strangely, things sharpen visually, / gather mass into themselves, hugging colour as though / their own physical limits were arms," he modestly claims, "I / haven't expressed it well . . ." In his poem set at a writers' retreat, Barry Dempster with his signature humour bemoans the difficulties of description: "See that leaf waving to the great below, / is it stop-sign red, no, lighter, rosé, / geez, can't one of us get it right?" Kildare Dobbs's poem "It" doesn't even attempt to reveal the antecedent of that powerful, ambiguous pronoun. Instead the poem describes the unease "it" causes. You might feel safe, the speaker advises, but "it is never far away / and it can be here whenever it chooses." There is no false attempt to describe what is indescribable, to make the invisible into a substantive. The poet resists an easy, felicitous naming. And for that reason, among others, we go to poetry where language gets dusted off, renewed, purified.

It is this scrupulous, engaging attention to diction, along with the sad acknowledgement that words can't be collared and brought to heel, that sets poetry apart from other genres and one poem apart from another. In a good poem the words are charged with a potency and precision that would be envied by the most punctilious scientist. Sometimes, as in Ross Leckie's "The Critique of Pure Reason," a poem conflates poet and scientist. "There is the intelligence of spruce needles," the poem informs us, "the way / they interlock and the way they enclose space / and make it intimate . . ." Jan Zwicky opens "Autobiography" with a meticulousness that avoids any fancy footwork or tropes: "In the years when winter snow piled up / along the edges of the streets, beneath the

windows / on the lee side of the hedge, / I did my homework at a
desk my father built." This kind of sharp particularity that places
the desk in its exact position in the house allows Zwicky to
move into
the more difficult and emotionally charged territory that the poem
steps into next. It is as if the speaker can compose only one image
after another, barren of metaphor or flourish. The last two lines
pummel the reader with the usually unemotive word "before." Re-
peated five times, its double meaning asserts itself: "before" is both
an adverb of position, as in "in front of," and a signifier of time. It
moves the nouns it precedes inexorably forward through the solid
world of things to the abstract: "Every morning / the light melts
the snow— / before books, before desks, before windows, / before
pain, before amazement."

Zwicky's poem reveals what images can do to vivify the intangi-
ble. Images, with or without metaphor, are as essential to poetry as
glass to a window frame. Listen to Armand Garnet Ruffo describ-
ing his aunt: "My aunt is in a western bar dancing. She throws her
cowboy hat / in the air, revealing her bald head." Sue Goyette gives
me a shiver when she writes, "This last lamp is held up to examine
the dark tongue of animal." And Evelyn Lau ends "Swimming
Lessons" with a sharp-eyed description redolent with implication:
"I struggled back to shore / where you stood, hand held over /
your eyes, looking in every direction / but this one."

If God is in the details, poetry is in the images. And then, there's
metaphor. Aristotle claimed that metaphor-making is a skill that
can't be taught. Metaphoric language, which includes the sim-
ile and metonymy, is a sacred trope. Its bringing together of two

unlike objects creates a newborn thing, not an invention but a discovery of something primal, something we have missed, as if the writer has pulled the string of a light bulb in an earth-walled cellar. A metaphor that is both apt and transcendent, that feels both ancient and novel, reminds us that all things are connected, even man and animal, dark and light, breath and not-breath. Metaphor spells out what Baudelaire called "the universal correlation." There are luminous examples in every selection in this book, but here are a few to whet the appetite for what poetry can do. In her address to the painter Mary Pratt, Katherine Lawrence pays tribute to the painter's gear—brushes, oil on canvas, linen. She then writes, "Your sable brush potent as a pig's snout, *Girl in a Wicker Chair* / the scent / of what we see." With his necromancer talents, Don Domanski turns fantasy into reality: "a little frost [is] haunting its own white hair." And finally, Anne Compton opens our eyes to see "By dusk, the forsythia's starting up: Its flash-blub / flowering, penetrative. Someone abroad with a jacklight."

• • •

The language of poetry does more than mean and more than solder one thing to another to make an exquisite, new-fangled fit that holds. Poetry takes us back to the sensory quality of the words themselves, their syllabics and accents, their sibilance, clicks, guffaws, and moans. Jim Johnstone's poem "Disgraceland" ends with the musical flourish I looked for in all the work I chose for this anthology: "a tongue / returning to the cave of its mouth, / the origin of sound. Ta-da!" You hear it in Rosemary Griebel's

"Wonder," in the lovely echoes of "moth" and "mother": "Deep in the brain, a moth-like shadow. / The moth in mother that makes her forget." The long o's of Warren Heiti add an alchemical music that enriches his philosophy: "and each thought is a spoke / in the solar wheel. But this / crocus is also its own idea / of whiteness . . ." The delight of Zachariah Wells's tribute to the Lyrebird lies in its playful rhymes and onomatopoeia: "trigger-snick / and barrel blast of shot that missed home." Music has its own audible intelligence. In fact, many poets claim that it is the music that helps them think their way through the poem. You can hear the melody weaving its threads of revelation in the rhapsodic, loping lines of Tim Lilburn and Karen Solie. In "Postscript," listen to her rhymes in a single, simple statement: "I went back, to the dirt track through the Ravenscrag / Formation . . ." Even Michael Johnson's Babuleo in "In Praise of the Village Idiot," with his anklebells, "his testes dangling / from torn shorts," and his inability to speak, wonders at the end of the poem: "Did I make music today?"

• • •

In the more than 150 issues of literary magazines I read for this anthology, I was looking for poems that had everything—sound and sense, a depth of feeling, and a wide-reaching, spark-inducing intelligence. I wanted to see an assurance of form, an accomplishment of cadence, poems that grappled with something significant, poems that mattered to the mind and the heart, poems that mixed the ordinary with the strange and uncanny. My work had already been done by the dozens of magazine editors who did a remarkable

job of sifting through submissions and choosing poems that sur-
prise and delight the reader. I congratulate them heartily, but their
sharp editors' eyes made my task harder.

Along with the constraint of size I tried, almost successfully, to
overcome the constraint of taste. When I reviewed the final lists, I
was delighted by the range of poets and poetry. I comforted myself
and, in advance, any dissatisfied reader with the knowledge that
next year a different editor will make different choices. One of
the things I admire about the series is its democracy, its freedom
to feature poets of long standing with those who haven't yet pub-
lished a book. At least half of the names I did not recognize; on the
other hand, some of those I included are writers who have received
numerous awards and who have appeared in major anthologies.
All of them made 2009 a glorious year for poetry fans when they
sent off their pages through slow mail or fast, allowing us to en-
gage with what was going on at a particular time and in a particu-
lar place, from Newfoundland to Vancouver Island, from country
to city and always, to quote Gerard Manley Hopkins, from the
mind's "cliffs of fall . . . / no man-fathomed," and the borderless
environs of the human soul.

Though most of the poems are written in open forms, there
are many that lean towards traditional structures like John Barton's
rhyming couplets, Carey Toane's thirteeners, Karen Solie's quat-
rains, Marilyn Gear Pilling's tercets, Rebecca Leah Păpucaru's cin-
quains, and Zachariah Wells's sonnet. Especially impressive is Mary
Dalton's formal tour de force in "Three Centos," in which she uses
the seventh or fifth lines of forty-five other poems to create some-
thing strange and original. I was pleased to include writing

Introduction

that blurs the line between poetry and prose: the lyrical paragraph of Sue Goyette, the Robert Bly-like field notes of Alan Cooper and Glen Downie, the brief lyric essay of Beth and Lenore Rowntree, the epistolary format of Katherine Lawrence, and the melding of lyric, story and language-critique in Lori Saint-Martin's "Quatre fruits/Four Fruits." Fiona Tinwei Lam's "Aquarium" and Eleonore Schönmaier's "Weightless" stand out for another reason. They're small, quiet poems, the kind that too often get overlooked for those that seem to be of bigger ambition or merit. In some ways, these two pieces speak most eloquently for the art of poetry in its purist form and for the alembic power of brevity. And standing as a rebellious, sassy argument against anyone's poetic rules, even a former poet laureate's, is Marilyn Gear Pilling's "Billy Collins Interviewed On Stage at Chautauqua." Among several admonitions, Collins asserts "you can't have people in your poems." Taking on the role of the rebel that every poet must ultimately be, Pilling ends her piece with Aunt Evelyn. How much she loved her, she writes, and "How proudly she wore her moustache / to church."

• • •

The name that sent a shiver up my spine when I came across it in my search was P.K. Page, one of Canada's most revered poets, who died at ninety-three on January 14, 2010. Over sixty years ago she wrote a poem called "Cullen." When the poem opens, Cullen is fifteen and in the concluding stanza he goes off to war. Decades later, P.K. returned to her eponymous hero, this time a fifty-year-old man, in "Cullen Revisited," a less interesting poem than the first. Now, as if she's decided to bless us from whatever country of the dead she resides in, she reveals his final chapter, the best poem in the trio, "Cullen in Old Age." In this resurrection, Page's character is ninety-two, and to his aged children's embarrassment and disdain, he who searched for solitude in his youth, who lived in an otherworldly state of dream and vision in his middle-age, now dresses oddly in shorts, baseball cap, and spurs, and more shockingly, marries for a third time.

The radical changes in the man are paralleled by the formal differences between the first Cullen poem and the last. In the final poem Page uses less rhyme and more rhythmic variation, so much so that the standard iambic pentameter line, the metrical pattern of the first "Cullen," is rare. This difference may simply be a reflection of Page's own loosening up of the stricter forms she mastered as a young writer, but it also mirrors the central character's disordered questioning about the afterlife and the existence of the soul. There is more wit in this poem, more leaping from certainty to ambiguity, from seriousness to humour. One stanza, significantly compressed into only two lines, sums up what Cullen's longevity has come to: "An empty page, he thought, surveying his life. A palimpsest— / illegible images glimpsed when he squinted his eyes." What a succinct, chilling conclusion made even more disturbing when we know that behind Cullen's words is a woman who spent her life creating images on a page.

It is the similarity between the poet and the older Cullen that ramps up the poem's remarkable achievement and its effects. The first Cullen felt like a fictional character, there to express some of the writer's concerns about modern life and its ennui. The second one was a bloodless symbol. This final Cullen is an alter ego. Like him, P.K. Page never lost her curiosity and her dazzling ability to catch what the senses have to offer and what remains beyond the reach of knowing and language. To her friend, the poet and biographer Rosemary Sullivan, she said near the end of her long and glorious life, "To keep living I need to write."

In an essay P.K. wrote in the mid-eighties, she describes the challenge of creation. Acknowledging that the senses are inadequate, the struggle is "to fit the 'made' to the 'sensed' in such a way that the whole can occupy a world larger than the one I normally inhabit." She achieves that larger habitation in "Planet Earth," a glosa in which she uses four lines from Pablo Neruda. It is a poem that asks us to treat the earth as a living organism, one that must be cared for and loved. "It has to be made bright, the skin of this planet . . . we must draw it and paint it / our pencils and brushes and loving caresses / *smoothing the holy surfaces.*" In 2001 the United Nations, as part of its Dialogue Among Civilizations Through Poetry, selected "Planet Earth" to be read simultaneously around the world, including in New York, at Mount Everest, and in Antarctica. The occasion honoured not only P.K. Page but also a rich and ubiquitous theme of Canadian poetry, the growing angst over our ruination of the natural world.

What are now called ecological poems carry the same attention to detail and setting as the nature poems of our literary ancestors, Bliss Carman, Archibald Lampman, Duncan Campbell Scott, and Pauline Johnson, but there's a new bite to the work, a palpable elegiac tone. A younger generation, writing concurrently with P.K. Page in her last few decades—Patrick Lane, Don McKay, Tim

Lilburn, Sharon Thesen, and Don Domanski, to name a few—
share her compassion, sadness, and anger, salted with a sense of
wonder for this world we inhabit and destroy. Along with the up-
surge in the number of species we have lost, the list of writers with
ecological concerns at the heart of their poetry continues to grow.
I came across them again and again in the hundreds of magazines
published in 2009 and felt compelled to represent them here.

Many of the new nature poems are urban like Glen Downie's
"Nocturnal Visitors," Sonnet L'Abbé's "The Trees Have Loved Us
All Along," Ken Babstock's "Lee Atwater in Blowing Snow," and
Nick Thran's "Aria with a Mirror and No Earplugs." As well, the
relationship between the animal and human is more complex than
in our country's nature poems of the early and mid-twentieth cen-
tury. The poems you'll find here are ones of praise, yes, but they
don't turn away from the messy and disturbing. At the same time,
there's a fresh, un-ironic sense of wonder in them, reminding me
of Rilke's adage that one must place one's hand on the earth like
the first human being. This quality is palpable in Peter Sanger's
"Sea Horse (for M.)," Paul Tyler's "Manitoba Maples," and Mela-
nie Siebert's "Ditch." Are these contemporary poets reminding us,
too, that we are perilously close to touching the earth and its many
marvels for the last time?

Embodying both grief and amazement and reminding us of
poetry's capacity for paradox, Catherine Owen's "White Sale" is an
exemplar of the ecological aesthetic. A salesman shows the speaker,
who is trying to buy an iceberg in the desert, the iceberg's blow
holes. She says, "sometimes when it's quiet, I press my ear / to
them like shells and hear the cold again." It is a poem of despair,

marvels the reader into a reified astonishment about the things and creatures of the world. Glen Downie's raccoon mother in "Nocturnal Visitors" took apart a watch "*in the dark* and licked its gears clean while her babies tied [his] shoelaces together." With subtle humour, Downie challenges the assumption that humans possess a superior intelligence. For the raccoons, "With the right piano, Chopin would be a breeze." Patrick Warner goes one step further. His poem "The Mole" makes it impossible to distinguish between the mole and the human. What visceral delight I feel when I read, "And blinking / by the swings on that suburban lawn / was my penchant for darkness and filth, / my penchant for sticking my nose in."

Anthropomorphism still exists in these contemporary eco-poems, but the poets here move into the danger zone of human subjectivity with a mad leap into hilarious hyperbole (Paul Tyler's "Manitoba Maples," for instance, "bulge into sewer veins, godzilla-limbs arching / over rooftops") or they tread into flora and fauna territory with a delicacy exemplified in Sue Sinclair's "Cherry Trees." In describing her reaction to the beauty of the blossoms, the speaker says, "It feels like someone has put their head / on my shoulder. And it weighs / nothing at all." In Allan Cooper's "Two Glimpses" the speaker observes a toad and "can just see his white throat moving in and out, slow as the pulse of the universe." The Judeo-Christian hegemony of the human is brilliantly and quietly deflated in Anne-Marie Turza's "Anthem for a Small Country." In the third of six couplets she writes, "As for religion, we peer into the drains and the old burrows / of earthworms, looking for the shyness of our shrinking god."

Lorna Crozier

The ecological poems in this anthology, though they confront in sad and vital imagery the sorrows our species has brought to the world, make me feel hope. It is a hope that has something to do with the enraptured concentration the poets have brought to their subjects and their joyous and evident delight in putting to use our soiled and cadenced Canadian English. The varied metaphors, images, music, and forms of these poems enact our planet's glorious though disappearing diversity, illuminated by the fire of poetic attention. The poets here open our ears to the pulse of the universe and our own hearts beating. They break open what we think we know and, in the cracks of that knowing, let in a different kind of light.

In his poem about his role as a movie double, David Seymour admonishes himself to "Pretend. Be unreal. / Be more real than I have ever imagined." Yes, I said out loud when I read those lines. He could be speaking for and to the fifty poets published here and those who care enough to read poetry. Jim Johnstone leaves poet and reader with an equally thrilling bit of advice. It's okay to forget the earth is flat, he says, for ". . . it bends / when you hold feathers in your teeth, / when you find the breath to laugh."

Lorna Crozier
SAANICH, BC

The Best Canadian Poetry in English 2010

KEN BABSTOCK

Lee Atwater In Blowing Snow

Strangely, things sharpen visually,
gather mass into themselves, hugging colour as though
their own physical limits were arms. I

haven't expressed it well, but spruce
in this park shoot skyward yet settle into a loaded, over-ripe
ur-green set off against the new, white,

puffed up, second tree each tree's
acquired. Fire hydrant in its bonnet and fox stole only glows
more vibrant gold and sits still. Every

humped thing plotting the graph of itself;
silent accumulation of secondary facts all pertaining
to a horizontal axis. The cast metal, bolted,

public bench, for instance, looks more comfy
now, with padded slats, though no one sits there. The waist-high
commemorative plaque's just another

memory beneath a growing drift.
It looks like cake. What I like is the foreknowledge
of gusts, blunt head winds. Pick out

Ken Babstock

the advance edge of a gathering front
before it arrives, stings and shocks your face away. Like
footage of a cloud of krill, or shoal

of silver fish, the white points stall mid-air
then alter course, shift, re-align and gather speed all synced
to a system of signals invisible from this chair.

Coleridge saw starlings flit and sweep
then climb and bank en masse and thought his mind resembled
them, kept him from finishing great

things he'd long ago begun. It wasn't
the opium. Shadows bloom, stretch, cat-paw across the blank;
it eddies in behind as I push on and mends

the clean glitter where I've punctured it.

4

JOHN BARTON

Mill Creek Reverdie

Whoever really loves abandons all sincerity.
—André Gide

Soil turned and thawed against your grass-stained chest—
face down in the rot with last fall's exposed

wind-felled leaves yellowed, tangled, and unkempt
in your loosestrife hair as, sun-starved, you press

into rank humus, desire's substrate danse
célèbre, me and you, young, one radiant

both erect—time's stand-in: prime Alberta
marble, your luminescent torso carved

from less glancing thoughts than mine, such arrows
I might have aimed to more useless import

had I sensed what I might not be, snow gone
crystal as it melts, love fleshed by sorrows

nameless as of then—what I could not feel
you would not know, facing down your ideals

set for harvest ahead of planting seed
while I go native in scrublands untreed

John Barton

by barren, suspect urges, the barrens
    of my eyes for you in bloom with sudden

        midges hatched among reeds in unfrozen
    sloughs, pollen furred on insect thighs flaxen

in arid pistils of parkland roses—
    what you'd expend in dirt not presupposed

        for waste, but as flowerings youth arouses
    through drives not mine to birth, so left unsown.

ANNE COMPTON

Heat in April

jacklight: a light used illegally as a lure when hunting or fishing at night

If you knew the end would you ever begin?

Of two people, one must be after—living
by praxis. Who's left behind lives another world,
not the old less one.
                          The perimeter daffodils—
a police tape circling the property. Its trees
quizzical in April light.
                          Here in the house,
an old certainty among cups rattles the cupboard,
and those six fabric buttons for your good shirt—
futile fastenings in a copper bowl.
In the woods, last year turning to leaf mould.

By dusk, the forsythia's starting up: Its flash-bulb
flowering, penetrative. Someone abroad with a jacklight.
Below it, the tulips, in thirsty abundance, cupping
the warm rain. There is something in us, after us.

ALLAN COOPER

Two Glimpses

1 THE TOAD

Here at my feet in last year's grass a toad has hunkered down from the wind. When I touch his pebbly back, he hunches down even further in the tawny grass. I can just see his white throat moving in and out, slow as the pulse of the universe. He is unassuming, practical, a small bag of stones left out in the sun to dry.

2 A PORCUPINE

When a porcupine wanders out of the goldenrod, what should we expect? One or two quills left behind, firm and slender and black. Look how the ink rises in the quill! We'll have to pay a lot for these gifts.

MARY DALTON

Three Centos

CLOTH

Carry water, carry water
and it too will be history. Out there
it helps, dead of winter, to have magnitudes

swell out and fail, as if a door
to the exit gate, or—if you stopped to look—
a mathematical question for your evenings.

The cats sanitize their wounds,
seem to remember seasons,
the will of an executioner, a crevice.

The screens yawn the bees through:
through the fog and the minute's silence.
Like a photograph, but not of itself.

Or did we only imagine that shape,
Odysseus with his many-skilled fingers?
Sister may be a blur, Great-Aunt a smear.

The fog won't lift tonight—
but now we are alone with it and know
a piece of cloth was lost beyond the line.

Mary Dalton

The notes abandon so much as they move,
and now it is the souring flowers of the bedraggled,
alone by the river with its mandolin.

And the young ones?
And another man, who remains inside his own house,
throwing a little tin pail at the heart of the priest.

On either side there's a wall
that holds up the huge doors and altars;
the screen door bangs and it sounds so funny—

the green-headed fly shouts as it buzzes past,
watching the landscape unravel into what's gone.
The ant's a centaur in his dragon world,

but when he finds that thin green seed,
branches agog with secrecies
that spring—

maybe he didn't make it. Maybe hydrogen—
people believe it, maybe from laziness.
And to participate with the flayer.

Three Centos

On a misshapen wheel
we play "What animal would you be?"
It must swim for miles through the desert,

the rocks,
the bestiaries of the ancients—
speechless with soil, and blind.

AUTOMATIC DOORS

And his mouth was an oil exploration gone bankrupt—
so much was paid
the dog tapped its tail.

Later, though, drawn together by
all those years of looking but not touching
the fabulous animal,

a coin in the tongue, I looked round for a cue
at the world of Business,
the automatic doors wincing away.

They got a lot of closet space
and each of them is inwardly a vault
that presses up and blunts

those who walk ahead even though the wind blinds them.
All over the roof rain hisses,
Who was your favourite? Who had a crush on you?

BARRY DEMPSTER

Mary Lake Writing Retreat

Late afternoon, Mary Lake, islands
dipping their fall poses in glass.
Five of us on the dock, semi-circled
in green plastic chairs, rumouring
over loons and deer, wondering whether
something might happen we could write about.
See that leaf waving to the great below,
is it stop-sign red, no, lighter, rosé,
geez, can't one of us get it right?
How about Chinese red, like the robes
in a Zhang Yimou swordfest, yes,
as perfect as human beings
who can't whoosh across the sky can get.
Five poems in the making, five shades of
Chinese red, one over-observed leaf.

Are writers competitive? a friend asks.
Wishing I could describe how we all
reached for the leaf as one stretch, like
Michelangelo's Adam multiplied. How
just before it hit the ground, another followed,
and another, perfect copies of
the same intention. We headed off in all
five directions, leaves tucked behind our ears,
poems spilling out like breadcrumb trails,
follow me, no, me, echoing
into the richly-described woods.

Barry Dempster

Later that night, draped in moonlessness
and searching for more, we almost bumped
into a deer posed beside the boathouse.
You're real, we said in unison
as he sidled into the trees and we
followed with our nets of reverence.
Each one of us reached out and touched
the darkness to our own soft parts: *so this
is what wild feels like.* As close
to speechless as we could be without
sacrificing our communal tongue.
Holy as a deer, we all would have written
in the notebooks we seem suddenly
to have mislaid somewhere.

KILDARE DOBBS

It

It was out there, occupied in the city,
But just now it was here, in the room with me.
I contemplate a bowl of big white blossoms;
with out-of-focus eyes I stare till they move
almost unperceived and soon it has made its
face from the white and the shadows and is now
a mask, looking at the floor and not at me.
I blink and it has gone, having made its point.
I think it was signalling, you are safe now
but just you wait, it is never far away
and it can be here whenever it chooses.

DON DOMANSKI

Gloria Mundi

To the sleeper, alone, the animals came and shone
—Josephine Jacobsen

early November   no narratives left
in the dead grass   backyards
beginning to hold our afterlives
a little frost haunting its own white hair
the dead envious   watching the endless
youth of dust settle on everything

bare trees weighted down with crows
and another planet's moonlight
a mouse's shiver in the fallen leaves
its pins and needles out of whack

shadows of the Pleiades under seven stones
feral cats moving about on paper cuts
no bats to sieve the air   no oracles
to predict what tenderness will do

the bodies of crickets lay ungathered
their prayers were like ours   cislunar
held in place by fear and doubt
never arriving at any destination

night came smoothly with a low growl
like the muscles of a bestiary pulling
its covers shut and the glory of the world
became disembodied   weightless
above your pure wish to be secure

bedtime and now the animals will arrive
claws and fur and geomorphic skins
all beside you   all warming you
with their bodies of switchback flesh
                          and rheumy bones

close your eyes   unclench your hands
dreams come through the maternal line
and clouds are our mother tongue
go to sleep   repeat after them.

GLEN DOWNIE

Nocturnal Visitors

They're not fooling anyone with those Lone Ranger masks, a disguise as thin as Clark Kent's glasses. But they're super with their hands—opening garbage cans, unwrapping fish guts—believe me, you don't know the half. They climbed down our tree one night while we were eating. My watch was drying on the picnic table after slipping off into the punch. Mom took it apart *in the dark* and licked its gears clean while her babies tied my shoelaces together. It keeps better time now than it ever did—a bit slow in the day, but always sharp at night. It's only the 9 to 5 that keeps them out of dentistry and the bomb squad. With the right piano, Chopin would be a breeze.

SUE GOYETTE

This Last Lamp

*Do not be deceived: this last lamp does not give more light—the dark
has only become more absorbed in itself.*
—Paul Celan

Like the deer running erratic in the mall, the dark is out of breath.
It's not that you're chasing it, more like holding up torches and

threatening to. It's good weather for a witch hunt and you don't
trust it, do you? This last lamp is held up to examine the dark

tongue of animal. What has it eaten and how does it talk? This last
lamp is a miner down the long throat of midnight. Your father sits

with his thermos, his legs not being what they used to be. Go on
without me, he says, and you do. What choice do you have but to

strike his gentle words like a match? The only thing that burns is
the lonely hour without him. Ah, grown up, how do you tell the

time? There is a wolf in your memory; when you wake, you see it
running with something in its mouth. Save the children, your

wife screams and you get out of bed and start the car before
realizing it was only a dream. The children are long gone, the stilt

Sue Goyette

of their shadows, a highrise towering over the rural plot you've
become, you a scruff of ragweed and thistle. Remember your

plans? And the candle you called yourself?

ROSEMARY GRIEBEL

Wonder

Here are the ones who wait in empty hallways.
The ones who watch time open and close the door.
The sky leans down, and a sun hard and yellow as tartar
Peeks in windows. No one wants to wake up.
Deep in the brain, a moth-like shadow.
The moth in mother that makes her forget.
Somewhere a photograph, and the slow heft of prayer.
Slippered feet and wool sweaters embroidered in flowers,
Lily of the valley and rose scent twined with catheters.
Soup, cream of. Biscuits and tea at three.
Out there, the pond's surface wrinkled with leaf tatter and wind.
The furrow and fluster fills the mouth with ash.
Creased maps of upturned palms, shawls heavy as wings.
To the quiet deepening, leave the silence to come.
To the young, leave the breadcrumbs of life.
This, the perfect emptiness that holds everything.

ADRIENNE GRUBER

The Rope

for Allison Cammer

Wind is something that holds us together, it doesn't push us
apart like some might think. We are tied to this place

by the almost. What could've happened, what almost happened,
what did. A man and a woman die from exposure

200 meters from their home. Exposure is a funny word,
drives us further into the storm. If someone ripped you

open right now and examined, they might be horrified.
Wouldn't want to expose too much. Especially not

the fear of what might happen. But you were safe
in your car the day of the storm, watching traffic

jam all the way down 20th as cars edged toward the
Broadway Bridge. Suddenly a city in crisis and you

full of energy for the first time in months. The radio
your only contact within this disappearing world.

A world turned white. No, not white. Dirty. The worst kind
of colour. Who we imagine ourselves to be

is nothing like how we turn out. There are families
who can't leave the Co-op and children

abandoned in schools. The Bessborough fills with those
who can't get across the river. A hundred years ago

these would have been deaths. Never lose grip on the rope
that holds the house and barn together.

JAMELLA HAGEN

Driving Daytona

They called it "Daytona," driving the same loop
        through town, over and over in Jeff's white van
with the rusted rear fenders and dirty carpeted interior
        the same musty shade of brown as every cheap
motel. There were three Hazeltons—Old Town, New
        Town, and South Town—Daytona was mostly
old and new, they'd turn up the music
        and you'd lie down in the back of the van
with the other girls. Cannibal Corpse, Deicide,
        Sepultura, the boys kept joking
they'd start their own Northern BC metal band
        called Chainsodomy. Shane wore a black T-shirt
every day that read *Butchered at Birth* with an image
        of bleeding skeletons lifting bleeding fetuses
from bleeding ribcages. You loved those boys,
        in your own way. Watched them try
to break beer bottles over their heads one
        after another. The bottles never broke and neither
did the picnic table they threw into the lake or
        the mood that settled in the morning after,
Shane hanging limp out the window,
        the van dragging heavy through gravel,
through queasy stands of poplar and cottonwood,
        hauling its sad sick cargo back to town.

STEVEN HEIGHTON

Some Other Just Ones

a footnote to Borges

The printer who sets this page with skill, though he may not admire it.
Singers of solo expertise who defer and find harmonies instead.
Anyone whose skeleton is susceptible to music.
She who, having loved a book or record, instantly passes it on.
Whose heart lilts at a span of vacant highway, the fervent surge
    of acceleration, psalm of the tires.
Adults content to let children bury them in sand or leaves.
Those for whom sustaining hatred is a difficulty.
Surprised by tenderness on meeting, at a reunion, the persecutors
    of their youth.
Likely to forget debts owed them but never a debt they owe.
Apt to read Plutarch or Thich Nhat Hanh with the urgency of
    one reading the morning news.
Frightened ones who fight to keep fear from keeping them from life.
The barber who, no matter how long the line, will not rush the
    masterful shave or cut.
The small-scale makers of precious obscurios—pomegranate spoons,
    conductors' batons, harpsichord tuning hammers, War of
    1812 re-enactors' ramrods, hand-cranks for hurdy-gurdies.
The gradeschool that renewed the brownfields back of the A & P
    and made them ample miraculous May and June.
The streetgang that casts no comment as they thin out to let Bob
    the barking man squawk past them on the sidewalk.

Steven Heighton

The two African medical students in Belgrade, 1983, who seeing
    a traveller lost and broke took him in and fed him rice and
    beans cooked over a camp stove in their cubicle of a room
    and let him sleep there while one of them studied all night
    at the desk between the beds with the lamp swung low.
Those who sit on front porches, not in fenced privacy, in the
    erotic inaugural summer night steam.
Who redeem from neglect a gorgeous, long-orphaned word.
Who treat dogs with a sincere and comical diplomacy.
Attempt to craft a decent wine in a desperate climate.
Clip the chain of consequence by letting others have the last word.
Master the banjo.
Are operatically loud in love.
These people, without knowing it, are saving the world.

WARREN HEITI

The Day

      The spring light is
palinodic. All that I've done,
I want to take back. The old
Eleatic master seems to think
the problem of participation
is about the just distribution
of stuff. But what if
an idea can't be
cut up and passed out
like a canvas sail? The day
is an idea and each thing
is thinking it, iridescently,
and each thought is a spoke
in the solar wheel. But this
crocus is also its own idea
of whiteness, the only dissent
in a consensus of purple.
The idea dies with it—but
that doesn't mean it can't be
known, an odour like coldness
from a garden hose, the song
of city water transposed
for the piccolo, an image
distinct as a six-eared star.
      At a sidewalk market,
the autumn spectrum

of apples: the sunset
has condensed in them.
It's beauty's accusation:
if you live your entire life over—
you'll never be equal to it.
I stand there at the corner, known
by the equinox and knowing
nothing, exposed by the alethic
light of those apples,
that fearless crocus,
the magnolia tree, its chandelier
of tears.

M.G.R. HICKMAN-BARR

Cattle Egret

You? I would peel you off,
gum on my shoe,
soft-stone—
like a knot started—
no stitching to follow, no
semblance of a pattern, or even
tiny needle pricks to advance
the fabric of a shared life.

Now
you are a language
spoken with a mouth sewn shut.
The syllables of your name
                              avoided
tongue gliding close
                    then
                        around,
like the speech by omission
of a menstruating Zulu woman
practising the avulsion
of her father-in-law's name.

I would bite my tongue bloody
than speak of you.

Yet still
you slender through
my thoughts.

Before—
thoughts crowded
like a herd of vibrant, patterned Nguni cattle,
enamelled white, red, brown, dun, yellow.
Startlingly wet-nosed,
pushing, trampling the distance
so carefully advanced . . .
and I, a white egret
who *follows the cattle* and *does not rest.*

Again
I gain ground,
each print fainter than the last—
first the toes
        lost,
then the surface of the mid-foot,
            lost.

The heels,
the plump balls of the feet—
as if I had never walked
your way.

MAUREEN HYNES

The Last Cigarette

The last cigarette burned up all my creativity
and resolve: that was the risk.
I had to do my own hiding now. Straddling
a huge whitewashed log on the beach
past Massett, facing the tip of the peninsula
where Raven cracked open the clamshell
to find men hungering to get out (there
were no women yet): that's where I smoked it.
In sight of Alaska. Ocean, sky, rocks, pebbles,
smoke—I drew all those shades of grey
deep inside myself, held them in
and felt my smallest cells come to life and expand,
from my lips down into my web of bronchioles. I exhaled,
followed the spiralling smoke up to the clouds with my tongue.
I asked the Hecate Strait to wash
the longing out of me, to release me
from the consequences of that addiction.
Incinerate the desire
to an ash. Pluck it out of me, Eagle,
and trick me blind, Raven. To make
my sacrifice tangible, I left my white
Che Guevara lighter on the log. Plastic, faded, but
treasured. I slid off the log, walked in up to my shins
over the smooth-washed egg-shaped stones,
casting my craving everywhere, into tide pools,
beside the sea urchins and electric blue starfish,

under enormous boulder walls
and into the cold, cold surf.

MICHAEL JOHNSON

In Praise of the Village Idiot

Torrents of sun from mica dust on the hedges
and driveway grass, the crushed-quartz drives
framed in avocados. Babuleo and his anklebells
long overdue. Rumour has him in a new shirt,
a jungle green. Rumour has him radiant.
It will not last, for he's not what we want
him to be. He spies through windows, eats
our garbage, goes about with his testes dangling
from torn shorts. Someone's sure to get him
new ones because they can't handle his immodesty,
his seeming care-lessness. They don't realize
he knows no other way. He sucks clay
because it tastes *good*, a saltiness he's found
no better than. And his garbage meals
shuck their ferment to his delight—all tasting
like gifts. His anklebells sound his coming
and kids badger him where he goes.
He seethes, curses them, their elusive ridicule,
their cruel normality. His gibberish
lends its own longing to the air, a palpable desire.
Desire that he could speak such words,
find the right invective, some sweet slang.
Desire that he could just talk. Then there are days—
today perhaps—when he finds a voice and sings;
a hollow rasping where his face speaks beauty,
blissful repose—a truce. He makes fluent sense,

Michael Johnson

a soulful parlance, like Beethoven to his own
deaf ear, as though he's always spoken perfectly,
never said anything else, as though he, even now,
was just wondering: Did I make music today?

JIM JOHNSTONE

Disgraceland

A highway at the end of the world.
The gluttony of a mouth . . . It's okay.

You can't be expected to remember
the earth is flat—it bends

when you hold feathers in your teeth,
when you find the breath to laugh.

We were doing well before Saint
Thomas Aquinas named five new ways

to sin—five hundred years of peace
brought us the cuckoo clock,

desperation oscillating on a pivot.
Here. Even in this lost heat

we wait for a wooden bird to appear
once an hour and rattle the quartz

in its breast. Whatever we see in those
seconds draws back, a tongue

returning to the cave of its mouth,
the origin of sound. Ta-da!

SONNET L'ABBÉ

The Trees Have Loved Us All Along

That trunk there is alive. Up out of a paved patch in the concrete sidewalk at Main and Broadway and strung with blue lights in the middle of summer, that trunk there is alive. I'm in its space. It doesn't give me a hard time about it. Putting my smells into its air, lifting my arms or not lifting my arms there is always still the crook from where my limbs branch from my trunk, the crevices and what moss gathers there. Fragrances. That trunk there is smelling everything, tasting everything through its body. Leaves like tongues, salivating, tasting my cunt right through my cotton underwear, my cotton denim skinny jeans, my crevices all hot for him and only the fibres of plants between all our nakednesses, his and mine and the trees', whose love filled me up enough to be able to breathe it out through the porous bark of my defences. Hard on the outside, raw pith in here, that trunk hears all the plants in our local designers' industrial looms and in the aching polished skins of our flirty shoes, all the fibres and minerals making bodies of themselves and loving themselves and standing there rough and unremarkable and plain green-leaved between the parking meters, knowing us, knowing us so well.

FIONA TINWEI LAM

Aquarium

Delicate, unworldly
seahorses behind the coral.
The grey one holds high
a noble, elaborate head.
The white one, belly full of young,
drifts near. Their tails entwine
as hands, even their unravelling
a slow caress. One hovers
while the other wanders
amid the anemones' waving tendrils.

Outside the glass,
my young son and I stand rapt
before this little paradise
as if it were a film
we must memorize
or perish.

His father has left us.
Probably for good.

EVELYN LAU

Swimming Lessons

The white doves flew in
and out of the trees below our balcony.
In our room we were fighting.
It was nothing, you said, *just a silly crack,*
it meant less than nothing—
a crack through which one moment slid
into another, swift as the sunset
in Honolulu. One moment the green Pacific
at our feet and then night,
sea and sky a thick blanket
thrown over the homes around Diamond Head.
The next afternoon the wave that knocked us both over
at Waikiki Beach stole my Fendi sunglasses—
and for a moment I wished
it had been a person instead, drowned
and swept away by the undercurrent, even someone
I knew but liked only a little, not like
I loved those glasses. The wave closed over
and over my head, I swallowed salt water
like medicine for a sore throat,
the sky suddenly miles above
and my body locked inside this watery room,
thrashing in a blue and airless bed.
So this was what it was like,
no time for remorse or reflection,
only an animal dying,

all helpless instinct and fear.
I struggled back to shore
where you stood, hand held over
your eyes, looking in every direction
but this one.

KATHERINE LAWRENCE

Dear—

(i) Dear Mary, Dear Mary Pratt,

Sable brushes, oil on canvas, linen—
the surface of all things a still life, *Red Current Jelly*, apples, bananas,
pudding, trout, *June Geranium* cuttings in a clear glass vase, water
line, sight line, scent

of chocolate cake, grilled salmon, wild violets, house on fire,
    another woman
on his fingers, *Donna*

is the lake at dusk, evening's catch gutted clean, the air redolent.
Your sable brush potent as a pig's snout, *Girl In A Wicker Chair*
   the scent
of what we see.

(ii) Dear Mary,

Aunt said a woman might contemplate a poem while ironing a
    basket of shirts,
a tablecloth, handkerchiefs, her comment its own kind of wrinkle.
    The iron is a triangle: one side for each person in a marriage.
    Steam his collar, trust the elemental—

Girl In My Dressing Gown, folds falling like pages, *It hadn't been pressed.*

(iii) Dear Mary,

It is nearly morning in Saskatchewan and an unmarried woman is in bed with a married man who visits her from Washington. He will wake in one or two hours and think: I love my wife. He will get out of bed without kissing the bare shoulder of the woman. He will go into the bathroom. She will open her eyes and listen to the sound of a man rearranging his life as he shaves. He will cut his chin. She will see herself as he saw her when they met: the outline of her shape in a white linen dress, string of red glass beads

Girl In Glitz, infidelity suggested by angle slope curve/waist hip
    thigh—

It is difficult to paint a person if that person is looking out of the
    painting . . .

Why did he choose his wife?

(iv) Dear Mary,

Narrative burdens the still life.

Read:
The Adulteress had prepared herself to love him:
She borrowed A Military History of America.
She lost eleven pounds over three months by not eating butter.

41

Katherine Lawrence

The man's wife worked in her studio all day but for a noon break: egg sandwich on brown bread, slices of orange, black coffee, *The Florentine*. A reader might infer: He missed his wife's lunches.

(v) Dear Mary,

We forgive but never forget—*I was touched by the marks of the buttons on her stomach and the impressions of stitches and zipper left by her jeans.*

Frame, wire, nail: After she had taken him to the airport, dropped him off at the Arrivals and Departures to save the expense of parking and other costs, greater costs, personal, she returned home, unlocked the front door, and stepped into the still life of her own persistence—oval braided rug, corduroy couch, hassock, glass coffee table, *Pomegranates In A Crystal Bowl,*
              . . . their colours shattered and reflected and re-reflected from one intricate surface to another.

(vi) Dear Mary,

Notes:
Italics indicate the titles of paintings by Mary Pratt, as well as commentary from her book, *A Personal Calligraphy,* Goose Lane Editions, 2000.

ROSS LECKIE

The Critique of Pure Reason

Is it that it is pure, that it is driven, that it is snow?
Snow in the reeds where I stand
as subject, as simple subject, as identical subject
in every state of my thought.
Winter cups its hands into time and freezes
it into a skim of ice. Time is partly opaque,
its pack of crystals occluding knowledge of the weeds.
They are at the bottom of the pond, beyond desire.
This is neither elegy nor ode. It is ice marked by the skate-edge of time.
I stand by my thoughts, here, at the edge of reason.
There is open water out toward the middle of the slough,
where the water birds congregate.
There I was a child in a photograph. I was the ancient of days.
I was the man who didn't have a ticket,
who waited outside, waiting to glimpse the performers
glissando from stage door to the waiting limousine.
It happened in the theatre of the trees,
hovering in shadow, the telos of snow.
I had to wait to hear the whole song,
because reason is shaped that way,
it has that kind of beauty, categorical. Look at the graph
the ridge of the mountains makes and there you will see it.
It is more true than accurate and more accurate than true.
The pond is in the shape of an "O" and if you make an "O"
in the moment before your solo, you're surprised
that you know its entirety as it knows the entirety of itself,

the song you can't get out of your head.
But there is no song in the world of reason, just the call
of a bird, just the breeze in the treetops.
In the quiet I can almost hear the reciprocity.
I expected it all to be reasonable, but I stood there
in the snow; we were reasonable beings,
the pond and the imagination caught in the ice,
the cattails and the wind of my breath,
the necessity of ice and the contingency of reason,
the tempered ice and the antinomy.
The pages are opening into the fields and the trees are pure reason.
There is the intelligence of spruce needles, the way
they interlock and the way they enclose space
and make it intimate, the way they brush the snow,
and in the snow, at this moment, time is all I have
to contemplate sunlight's interrogation of shadow
and the encroaching night's critique of sunlight
and that is how I know two plus two.

TIM LILBURN

Rupert's Land

Wolverine Creek de-caves, walks in its underwear from memory,
    then sets
itself in the wounds of Last Mountain Lake, where pelicans are,
                                                papery breath
of their glide.
And Last Mountain Lake gives what it's done, its rehab notes,
    endless antibiotic dripline of
weeds, all its clothes and shoes, to the Qu'appelle River and the
    Qu'appelle
lays its money inside the body of the Assiniboine (into its side), river
                                cranking, with an avocet's hitch,
from Ft. Pelly area, Kamsack, town of Enterprise, from the widefaced,
testosteroned stare of the Minichinas Hills.
Most of our courage slants wrong.
West, the stone Cabri Man rustles in poked and stirred light on
    salt plains.
Medicine wheels (quiet, move slowly now), saged-in pits on
    lunged hills.
Suncor waste ponds rebound bearings of day lost at a supreme
height, near the Athabasca where the river
packs its staked ass north.
Wolverine Creek tucks its nose below its tail
and the night can lance in around it.

Tim Lilburn

*

Suncor hired the guy who invented the guitar, a turtle-in-a-
    handbag
kind of daemon, cattle rustler, Mac the Knife.
He slid his put-on-backwards, hoofy shoes
on the glass floor.
No one had ever heard of shoes
used like that before he did it, nose in the groin of the wrong way.
Stupid cattle followed.
Religion grew to his lip like salmon lice.
On one knee before air audiences, the yet again Wayne Newton
    impersonations.
The swollen trident flew by this one's look into the water's neck.
A little underage, he carried his own cradle,
tucked in horsey blankets various moustaches, goatees and
    driver's licences.
Hermes, the beloved.
He gores the strings heavily every night in trailers in all the camps
chasing chords, blowing on banked coals, in Rolling Stones songs,
charming the oil from the sand.
He's seen moving in lamp light behind skin
windows in traders' sunk cabins at Île-à-la-Crosse, High Level,
    Ft. Chipewyan
heaved over, enpenned as a scorpion, inflamed with attention,
    tilting the old accounts
this way then that, his man-falling-from-a-building eye,
smoothing, smoothing the columns' singing flows.
Memory is the sweetest part of his heart.

Rupert's Land

*

Flanged rainclouds jackknife and wreck up in first air southwest
    of Dawson Creek,
mile 0, the Golden Road,
diesels churning, eddying, motionless in motel parking lots and in
front of the laundromat with showers,
the air's burnt coffee.
Muskeg swamps sulk north.

At Fort Nelson the two-year-old within his pack of dogs raises a head
beside a flag of Labrador tea three hundred yards from the high
    school football field
five hours after the vanishing from the backyard, dogs weaving liquid,
movement-suturing him in.
3:00 a.m., the twenty-year-old female,
well-oiled, passed out in the street,
shorts at half mast, the limp and saved offered
as apple slices on a blade.
Swallows carve something not seen
above Muncho Lake near the Lodge eaves,
lanks of air slithering away next to each flight curve,
hung meat cut.

Tim Lilburn

*

People like small piles of smoke on the South Gataga River
wait for orange food packs to drop in,
ghostgang rain tumplines across the hip of the Muskwa-Kechika range
and over the water's ridged, flipping back.
Sour gas wells flare in wind pelt somewhere, you can be sure, near.
Force blooms a torn black front eating east.
Logging roads hack up by thickset washes, the float plane sways
through
bullfields of mountains
into the lowest layer where shale-backed, fossil-tagged dragonflies
scale and scrape air
and a horsefly is caught in the fold of my shirt, August
heat.
Loons, vowel soaked,
their language expertly deboned
of consonant have come to invent the thinnest possible dusk,
handsome cold-pounded to sorrow, so that an obsidian razor leaps
at a bell rope falling the center of us.
In the morning, after a night of their cries, three
come toward me,
diving.

Rupert's Land

The mountains set their tables, above the snow,
in minimum light of end-of-night wind.
Granite and shale and rag of glacier.
Toad River, slate-milky—
armpit pain, ache in the jaw—
twists under us.
A marine fossil lodges in the north bank,
plume of a horn floating from front bulge to where an anus
    would be
at 113 Mile Creek, saw marks at one corner, up a side, fireweed,
    the underwater grass
milled to red above stone.
Memory is the sweetest part of his heart
and he's into collecting.
Horse tail clouds jackknife and wreck
up in wind sideswipe in the Muskwa-Kechika, mountain's
names kept away in beaded pouches
mountain's names left behind in braided grass boxes.

DAVE MARGOSHES

The Chicken Coop

The house my parents had built
for them went back to the bank
and we moved three miles down
the road to a chicken coop converted
to a crude home, and that's where I
learned first to crawl, then
to walk. Later, we moved deep
into an orchard of apples and pears
to an abandoned farmhouse
with a pond and snapping turtles
and eels. No chickens but geese
chasing the dogs with their eel necks
curved and it's here that I learned
to run, to talk, that I became the first part
of what I am. My father never overcame
his sadness at the loss of the house
he'd first drawn on a napkin at the Automat
on Lower Broadway—the house was gone
but he still had that napkin, crumpled
in the dresser drawer where he kept
folded money and his glasses. "It doesn't matter
how many new floors, how many coats
of paint," he would complain in his glass
of port, "you never get rid of the stink
of chickens." And he'd point
an uncertain finger at me. "Don't you
forget that. It's who you are."

JIM NASON

Black Ice

It was the laneway in January that frightened me most;
the reaching-out branches of leafless trees; rumblings
of the all night streetcar; the one or two people walking
through the dark and the snow stirring: all as it should be
when you have something to hide. It was the cold, grey
clouds; and framed in a square of light, it was the man
in the second floor window yelling at someone
I could not see. It was the way his fists pounded
the air and his shirt was off, thrown over the back
of a chair; the man was lean, his pounding and pointing
unyielding. It felt as if the someone was me, unsteady
on my feet. It was the falling, darkness and falling,
the time-crested glow of the moon reflected
in a sheet of ice and the thud that I heard was me
on my side looking up through the cold. It was
the light gone from the window and silence
except for the occasional streetcar rolling by.
It was the lane changing, deepening its shadow,
and I wanted to pull the ice like a blue-black
blanket over my feet and legs and fall asleep
because sometimes sleep is vertigo, the drawn-out
stutter of a radiant heart, the shifting plates of darkness.
It was stars, the upside-down naked-with-trees laneway at night.

CATHERINE OWEN

White Sale

when I tried to buy an iceberg, that day
in the desert, the salesman was dubious.
it had been a long time since he'd seen one
of those, he said, and the people had since
evolved, into sand dollars, into strange
kinds of fish. the ablation of glaciers
was complete. people bobbed like small
shoals of bullets in the flood, or squeezed
into cracks on the lengthening plains.
other species had vanished, sinking fast
on their pinions of ice, waving tiny attachés
of the future. we strolled on the moraine, he
& I, the now irrelevant spit that had once
held back the sea, and the land was split
with fissures, blood surrounding its mouths,
uncanny and rich as berries. those are the
icebergs' blowholes, the salesman nodded,
sometimes when it's quiet, I press my ear
to them like shells and hear the cold again,
the four-fifths of what we've forgotten, held hard
beneath.

P.K. PAGE

Cullen in Old Age

Cullen, at ninety, curiously attired—
shorts and a frock coat, baseball cap and spurs—
symbols, he said, of a life he'd lived forever
and ever and ever—(or so it seemed from here—)
took it upon himself to marry again.
His grandchildren rose, protesting.
"Silly old fool," they said, embarrassed.
"Give us a break."

"What do they know? Just what do they know?" he said.
"Puerile passion is puerile passion. Mine
is the work of a lifetime, one that includes the stars
and the depths of hell. I offer my laden heart
filled with a multitude of moons and suns,
and clouds as dark as thunder. All are hers
to do with whatever she will. She is my love."

"In for the money," his children said, uneasy
about the girlfriend.
Far too pretty. And young.
"In for the money and in for the kill," they said.
And wondered about his will.

When would he die? he questioned, unafraid
but interested.
There were all those friends

who had gone before, who knew what he didn't know.
Life after death? Extinction? He would like
to know this ultimate riddle before he died.

The Gospels, of course said, yes, the soul survived.
But has anyone seen a soul? Deep in the eyes?
No one he knew, although he believed they'd tried
to weigh it, by weighing the body before it died
and immediately after death.
Like weighing smoke, he said, or weighing air.
"The king of nothing is nothing," it seemed to prove.

*

An empty page, he thought, surveying his life. A palimpsest—
illegible images glimpsed when he squinted his eyes.

*

Cullen, in extreme old age could dream—
his best activity, the most exact
and most mind altering of all the drugs
he in his young and turbulent years had tried.
Clowns could appear, and queens, a whole parade
of children in paper hats, and dancing dogs.
Space could divide, like the Red Sea. As for time—
infinitely fracturable. Up or down.
Nanoseconds not in it. None could guess

Cullen in Old Age

how slow or fast that airy machine could travel
back or forward, or hover—a hummingbird.

He slept for a week, and obsequies were sung
in the heads of his heirs, and when he at last awoke,
pink as a baby and talking in strange tongues,
they wrote him off as crazy.
He was not.

On the stroke of four the Guardian Angel spoke
in pure Angelic, "Time, gentlemen, please."
But Cullen, not yet packed, and deaf as a boot,
was far from ready or willing to shut up shop.

He was a fossil, they said, a has-been, he
had lost his Elgin marbles, poor old creep
but he gave them a look from his ice-blue eye that froze
the marrow within their bones. He said, "The world
has made of itself a carnal shop."—A what?
" 'Sex and the Maiden,' " he said, "a Schubert song
that nobody knows today. Hip hop, hip hop."
A long and agonized wail came out of his mouth.
The cats, as if scalded, ran, and the ancient dog
barked to protect the house.
Cullen, not ready to die, not quite alive
outlived his third wife. Had a vision of heaven.
Total immersion. Where? He couldn't tell.
A flotation tank, perhaps, a void, a vast

container for single souls that gathered together
and merged in a giant soul that encircled the world
where everything came out even.
Linearity no longer a question, past
and future a part of time eternal.

Cullen slept, content, his life was spent
like a silver coin that slipped from a hole in a pocket.

REBECCA LEAH PAPUCARU

Rosalind Franklin in Open-Toe Sandals

Her bare legs and open-toe
Platform pumps are what you
Notice last in the photograph
Of the young crystallographer
At the conference.

First her hair, dark and loose.
Then her smile. The blouse open
At the throat. Even in black
And white you can tell she
Is still tanned from hiking the Alps.

She is on our right, about to open
The door. The men on the left are next,
In shadow, but then Rosalind
Is on the first step, and in their light.
Nine years before she dies,

She has come to Lyon
From Paris where she works for fellow
Jew Mering at his convivial lab:
A different photo shows her in checked
Shirtwaist, hair in a loose chignon,

Holding two Petri dishes full of the coffee
They brewed in beakers.
How could she not see the structure of DNA
Was a spiral staircase for inbred debutantes
To descend? How could she not spot the base pairs,

Reproducing without end, facing
Each other like inverted mirrors?
Photograph 51, the first glimpse
of DNA's helix. Rosalind took it
With the same X-ray machine

She had used in Paris.
When she saw that X-ray of her
Ovarian tumour, it seemed
Benign in comparison.
But that day in the Lyonnais sun:

Rosalind Franklin in open-toe sandals,
Foot firmly on the first rung.

MARILYN GEAR PILLING

Billy Collins Interviewed On Stage at Chautauqua

Billy Collins says you can't have people in your poems.
It can only be you and your reader.
You think of all the people in your poems:

your Aunt Evelyn, your mother, your friends Linda
and Dick and Ross. John Porter.
Your mother, your mother. Billy Collins says your job as poet

is to give your reader pleasure. You thought giving pleasure
was your job in sex.
Your reader's crotch is the one thing you never

worried about. Billy Collins says sometimes he takes his penis
off when he writes a poem.
You wonder what his penis does when it knows its master

is writing. Goes to bars? Appears for Margaret Atwood
as a remote-signature pen?
Billy Collins says strangers don't care

about your thoughts and feelings. You want to put up
your hand, tell him
about the woman behind you: you came

an hour early to sit in the front row and discovered
you'd forgotten your reading
glasses; you were so desperate at the prospect of an hour

doing nothing that you turned around and asked a row
of strangers if anyone had extra
reading glasses; the woman behind you lent you her brand

new pair. But he's back on pleasure. He says how you give
your reader pleasure is form.
Dusty old form! Grade ten sticking-to-your-varnished-

wooden-seat iambic pentameter! You're still
mulling that when Roger Rosenblatt
asks Billy Collins why he didn't become a jazz musician.

Billy Collins says he wishes he had become a jazz musician,
he wouldn't have to be on stage
answering these questions. So much for that

egg-over-easy persona of the poems, eh? Now he's saying
no decent poet ever knows
the ending of a poem he's writing. You think sadly

of all those endings you thought of in the shower, even though
you know Billy Collins won't care
about your feelings and you know you shouldn't use

an adverb in a poem. Then Roger Rosenblatt asks Billy Collins:
What is the importance of poetry?
Billy Collins sits up straight and says, Poetry is optional.

That's right, reader. Billy Collins, former Poet Laureate
of the United States of America
is sitting here on stage saying poetry is optional. And you

thought people died for lack of what is found there.
Wait a minute. Something's happening
on stage. Billy Collins is fed up. Billy Collins is leaving.

Unclipping his wings. They're black, just so you know,
like his suit. Billy Collins has the wingspan
of a frigate bird. There he goes—rising, rising, riding

the currents of institutionalized sublimity. Beating his way
across the ceiling beneath the track
lighting, brushing the Stars and Stripes aside. He's off to find

his roving mojo. You sigh and think about going home.
You'll have to rub out
all those people in your poems. You'll have to have a cold

shower whenever you feel an ending coming on.
You think sadly—
okay, adverbially—about your Aunt Evelyn.

How much
you loved her. How proudly she wore her moustache
to church.

LENORE & BETH ROWNTREE

7 lbs. 6 oz.

Some things about my sister Beth
that I can't think about for too long
without getting sad and confused:

1. The time we went to the Bracebridge
Dairy for cherry pie and vanilla ice
cream and she took too long in the
bathroom, so I kept knocking on the
door, and when she emerged she said,
"My life is hard, you know."

2. The time I blew snot out my nose
and rubbed it in her hair in front of
the boys from down the way who
were already afraid of her.

3. The time my cousin said at the family
reunion that she ruined everything.

4. The time some kids threw snowballs
at us on the way home from school,
and the ones they threw at her had
stones in them.

5. The time a man gave her an engage-
ment ring that was too big for her
finger so it came off during the night
in her bed, and the staff at the group
home found and returned it to the
man, who'd spent his disability
allowance on it, and she thought he
had broken up with her because she
lost the ring, and nobody ever told
her anything different.

6. The time I looked in her purse and
found nothing but scraps of paper so
covered in writing there was hardly
any white left on the pages.

7. The time my mother told me she had
a normal birth weight, 7lbs. 6 oz.,
but an abnormal delivery because a
bully nurse shoved her back in and
held her until the doctor arrived.

8. The first time she became an
outpatient at the Clarke Institute of
Psychiatry and wrote this list to
remember the layout:

7 lbs. 6 oz.

11th floor
Dr. Jeffries' Office
9th floor
8th floor
7th floor
6th floor
5th floor
4th floor
3rd floor
Day Care Centre
Ground Floor
Chapel

9. The time I found her poem "Lies" in
her wastebasket:

Happy
Jolly
Jovial
Pretty
Funny
Beautiful
Cheerful, Pleasant
Lovely, Sense of Humour
Educated, Famous, Smiling
Lies, Full of Lies, A Wheat Sheaf
    Full of Lies.

BETH & LENORE ROWNTREE
(photo by Gideon Rowntree)

ARMAND GARNET RUFFO

The Tap is Dripping Memory

My mind is a town with Main Street looking
like it's had its teeth punched in.
Its eyes blackened. Broken windows and empty lots.
And, then, it's a bright Saturday morning, and
I'm riding my bike down to the beach.

My parents relax on creaky lawn chairs.
I can hear their every move. They are in the shade
of a house made of bone and tar paper.

My sister is screaming the house is on fire. We run
to the Japanese neighbours. Exiles like us, my mother whispers.
In their tiny kitchen, we drink cocoa where everybody is safe.

My aunt is in a western bar dancing. She throws her cowboy hat
in the air, revealing her bald head.
Everyone turns away except me.
Then my sister says she doesn't want to die,
but she dies anyway.

I am ten again. We go for a family picnic, and I get car sick.
The dust from the road in my hair, clothes, mouth.
When we arrive I jump into a lake,
and find I can't swim. My father drags me out.

When we return a neighbour is skinning a bear on his back porch,
as if it's something he does regularly.
The bear is staring at me. His eyes get bigger and bigger,
until they become moons.

I arrive at a friend's door just in time to overhear him
say I swear and don't believe in sin. His parents
tell him I'm just a little pagan.
I creep away trying not to be noticed, but the floorboards
thunder with every footstep.

At home my dog Chopper is smiling at me with a curled lip,
and I am loving him in a moment so perfect the world opens for me.
The moment is a silver hook cast into a bottomless lake.
Floating until it sinks.

It's true. Some memories cannot be turned off with sleep.
I jolt awake, go for a glass of water, pull the curtains aside.
The light in the yard beside the tree is hard yellow.
The dripping tap punctuates the night.

LORI SAINT-MARTIN

Quatre fruits/Four fruits

*The pieces published here are reworkings rather than translations or
adaptations of a French sequence of pieces first published in* Liberté. *At
the request of* The New Quarterly's *editors, the first of them includes
the French alongside the English since the theme of it is the way one's
identity is changed when one's lover does not speak one's own language.
I see the changes made as intrinsic to the language I was writing in
and suggest they be read not as discrepancies or mistakes but as signs of
linguistic difference. I consider both versions to be originals.*

I

Mon amant ne connaît pas ma langue, mais je connais la
sienne. La mienne est vieille, cérémonieuse, la langue douce et
triste et gracieuse de la diplomatie et de l'amour. Sa langue à lui
résonne, tape, le pouvoir et la science, les troupes dans le désert, le
poing fermé. Sa langue est internationale, la mienne ne l'est plus.
J'ai appris, lui pas. Forcément.

Mon amant est professeur, spécialiste de mon pays; il veut
m'apprendre, douce leçon. Je ne veux que le plaisir que nous nous
donnons, brûlure, fête, luxe, une poignée de cerises parfaites, au
plus amer de l'hiver.

J'ai donné une conférence dans ma langue, dans sa ville. Il m'a
écoutée sans comprendre. Que des rythmes, un regard. Lorsqu'on
ne comprend rien, dit-il, on saisit bien la voix.

Mon amant ne connaît pas ma langue, mais je connais la sienne.
Il a essayé, pour moi dit-il, de s'y mettre. Peine perdue, il massacre
chaque syllabe, même celles de mon nom. Il a changé mon nom,

l'a absorbé dans sa langue. Il m'a absorbée, changée. Pour lui, oui,
je veux bien changer.

Je me fais fluide, mobile, voix-caméléon. Nous nous voyons,
quelquefois : des chambres nous attendent, dans son pays, dans le
mien. Quand je me réveille dans ses bras, au plus noir de la nuit,
je sais toujours où je me trouve. Je sais quels mots prononcer, dans
quelle langue d'amour et de chaud sommeil.

I

My lover does not speak my language, but I speak his. Mine
is older, softer, the sad, graceful tongue of diplomacy and love.
His rings out, brash and strong: money and science, troops in the
desert, a fist. His language is international now; mine no longer is.
So I have learned, and he has not.

My lover is a professor whose specialty is my country: he wants
to learn me, absorb me, a secret lesson. I want only the pleasure we
exchange, fingertips, skin, night ceremonies, a handful of cherries
at winter's heart.

I gave a talk, in my language, in his country. He listened
devoutly, understanding not a syllable, charting rhythms, a
cadence, a look. He says: only I listened to your voice, not your
words. (Love without understanding: a sweet dream.)

My lover does not know my language, but I know his. For
my sake, he says, he has tried to learn. Still he murders every
sound, even my name. He has changed my name, turned it into
something else. He has absorbed me, changed me, after all.

For him I am fluid, floating, chameleon-voiced. We meet, sometimes, in a room in his country, or in mine. When I awaken in his arms, in the dark of night, I always know where I am. I know which words to speak, in which language of darkness and of lovers' sleep.

II

For as long as their secret story has lasted, they have been meeting in this green and yellow 50s diner. Each time, on her way in, she picks up slices of lemons and limes from small white bowls on the counter. When they kiss in the room, afterwards, he tastes their acid freshness on her tongue. This love does not take their appetites away; they do not pine; it is a craving, an indulgence. The more they eat, the hungrier they grow. And yet today his eyes do not meet hers. In a voice she has never heard, he tells her it is over.

In a white saucer lies a thin slice of lemon, still intact. On the wall beside their booth is a poster of a famous painting: a green and yellow diner in a dark street, three customers bathed in fluorescent light. Their restaurant is identical, no doubt a copy. A man and a woman are sitting at a counter, side by side. Their pose invites storytelling, and she has chosen hers: a current of desire connects them, holds them fast. His hand just skims hers as he leans towards her, his hidden left hand resting, perhaps, on the red silk of her thigh. Her eyes are closed, pleasure turning inwards. At the other end of a counter a second man, seen from the back, watches the scene unfold. Desire eliminates distance: that is the story the painting has told her, since their meetings here began.

It's over, he said, we can't see each other any more. She has felt the wrong hunger, told herself the wrong story. The woman in the painting stares at her own nails, self-absorbed, heartless, miles away. The man is looking into space, or out towards the street where other figures pass.

The intimacy of flesh and skin is a lie, a dream. Although they are nearly touching, elbow to elbow at the long counter, there is nothing between the man and the woman, nothing at all.

III

"Saturday we are making jam." One thoughtless sentence and she sees it all: pale wood in the kitchen, copper pots, French doors thrown open to welcome the garden in. Roses and grass, dazzling light, and a brown-haired woman slicing strawberries in two, exposing their pale, fragrant hearts. On her left hand a gold ring shines, a ring she has worn so long it is hers in the way her nails are, the way her bones are. The man steals a berry and kisses the back of her neck, she shivers and begins to laugh. They exchange a glance; the moment burns. Married bliss: this is what it looks like. She knows the image is all wrong (the man loves another woman, loves *her*), but it cuts through her like a truth. Only truth can hurt this much. Hands on her lap, she waits for him, still and small in the slow dusk.

IV

He was waiting for her in Paris, in a small hotel on rue Madame. She was young and loved books, he was old and loved listening to her. So she talked and talked, she told him about Gertrude Stein and Colette, about the war and the salon on rue de Fleurus, close by.

He was returning from a business trip to Asia, she arrived from Montreal where they both lived. Paris was new to her then, though she would later visit dozens of times, without him. From Thailand he brought her mangosteens. Taste this, he said, you'll see.

The flesh was a clear, intense white cradled in a deep red skin. It tasted of calm and of sweet water, of distance, of a hidden spring. She had never seen the fruit nor heard the name. She was so young she still thought she would travel again and again with the same man, this man she confused with fate.

Ten years have passed, and she has never tasted anything so good since. Nor has she ever expected to. Ten years have passed and yet she sees the room, the open bed, the open fruit. She smiles, confident still and young, as if she had only to reach out her hands to have drop into them, one by one, all the fruits in the world.

PETER SANGER

Sea Horse (for M.)

Hippocampus, not hippo-
potamus. The ark
didn't bounce and recover
one handsbreath of freeboard
when you disembarked. If
Lamarck was right, by then
you'd refused the task
we now assume of being invariably
big. You flipped
yourself over the rail,
rode the tail of a salty brook
swallowing itself into ocean.

Unlikely as art, or the size
of a thumbnail sketch,
you keep the continuous arch
of a chess knight. All your
moves are upright, steering
by two rounded fins where your neck
swells down into what might
have been shoulder if you'd had
our recourse to arms. Instead,
you inhabit eelgrass and seaweed
where we might observe you approach
an amphipod in a casual manner,

peer at it a second or two
and placing your pipestem snout
in the most convenient position
suddenly engulf your meal. You
are said by those with the patience
to listen to make a monotonous sound
akin to that of a tambour
which becomes (understandably so) more
intense and frequent in breeding season
when a female deposits one hundred
and fifty eggs in a male's
ventral brood pouch. This marsupial

solution makes you fish, bird,
mammal. Practising such finesse
why did you ever reject
the amphibian? A male marsupial
who carries all her eggs in his basket
could only have had an enviable future.
As it is, you're seaside prelude to Ovid,
and we also did best to begin by inventing
Westminster Abbey. Later times will find
leisure and bombs to destroy it.
Sea pony, salt crystal, gallop me home,
mare, maris, marriage-maker.

ROBYN SARAH

Messenger

Little stone in my shoe,
what have you to tell me?
That such a tiny irritant can serve
to undermine a meditative mood
hard-won from day's commotion
by a walker on the mountain?
That I am obstinate, who will not stoop,
or stop to teeter on one leg
and tug at sandal-straps—
prefer to hope you'll work your way
out, same way you sidled in,
without my intervention?

Are you a stowaway—fugitive,
or just adventurer
hopping a ride to town,
a roadside pebble with big-city dreams?
Are you a terrorist—dispatched
to tell the plight of kindred
tired of being trodden on?
Are you a grain of sand,
seed for a pearl to my oyster brain?
Are you an augurer?

You cling and dig in
even to toughened skin,
and will not be appeased.
Little stone in my shoe,
what makes me choose
to walk with you awhile?
What little creeping guilt
accepts it as my lot
that you should harry my sole
the whole way home?

ELEONORE SCHÖNMAIER

Weightless

At the water's edge
is an empty canoe
open to the pouring

in of starlight;
it's inconceivable to bail
the light out

once it has been
(however briefly)
carried—

DAVID SEYMOUR

The Photo Double

On the gimballed replica of the tall ship
the director's face is lost behind a megaphone.

The cameras, correctly aligned, produce a seamless
waterline between the shooting tank and the Pacific
ocean behind it. Cloudy skies are ideal for this illusion.

Study the dailies, learn his moves. I am the mirror left
after the actor has used the mirrors up. The wide angle lens.

The scene requires the release of several thousand gallons
of siphoned sea water. De-commissioned jet engines
fill the sails on action. It will run 15 on-screen seconds.

There's a delicacy born of dangerous
moments the producers are desperate to capture.

View playback. The lead's on deck comportment
is casual, loaded with unrelinquished energies
cocked in slumped shoulders and languid, gorilla-like arms.

Tenderness confines its gestures to near misses, the use
of violence must always appear a life-saving measure.

David Seymour

Last looks. Final touches. An air horn blows.
The extras are miming. As the rubber sabre
strikes my arm I'll react like it's cleaved to bone.

Which has less to do with feeling pain
than understanding timing. Apply glycerine tear.

In the background all the British sailors
are Americans, all of the French are Mexicans.
Esta muy contento d'estai. Return to the dailies.

Now, when I'm alone I often act
as though someone else were watching.

Each take costs fifty grand. And the extras
continue to disappear, every time they leave
the picture frame. Cut. Cut. Camera reload.

They are about to roll again. Pretend. Be unreal.
Be more real than I have ever imagined.

MELANIE SIEBERT

Ditch

Strange how we go on looking in the lessening
light, along the highway, looking for the things thieves pitched
from the smashed windows of our van as they drove and rifled through:
maps, gospel cassettes, ball gloves, receipts and sermon notes,
sleeping bag and candles, scattered over miles, deemed
worthless, the ditches deep with grass, unmown. We're steeped
in the overrun, the laid low, the pooled and going nowhere,
in the tremolo of early evening, mint-tinged,
damp to the knees, even weeds and beer cans gleam
as if belonging here: we are intent, walking
without speaking, bending to gather each thing
as if it had a broken wing, might have flown but landed
wounded in the tall grass, beating. Strange how we go on
as if things matter, as if this were a place
where something essential could be found.
Cars blow by. A whistling cowbird bends
a tattered reed. We follow the light-licked
papers sailing above the grass, the field encroaching,
last winter's road-salt leaching down.

SUE SINCLAIR

Cherry Trees

A blur of white, pre-photogenic.
Ships bound for distant shores.

A hint of nostalgia
that isn't an escape—or if it is,
we escape only into the here and now,
only into this same place
cast in another light.

The trees stand unblinking,
pull down so much sunshine they seem
finally to disappear into it, become
a deficiency, pale, forgetful.
They gather absence around them
and are strangely increased by it
in a way I envy.

It feels like someone has put their head
on my shoulder. And it weighs
nothing at all.

KAREN SOLIE

Postscript

Two hours on that road, and we saw no one but jackrabbits,
those innocents of plane and direction who seemed compelled
from the middle distance, magnetized to the undercarriage.
All creatures are plagued by dangerous ambiguities

that inhabit the visual realm. If approached from the east,
an old community hall at an unmarked intersection
will summon its will and say CRANDALL. From the field where
that village stood, a farmer on his mid-century Case

waved to the car as if from one of the four corners
of the known world. The first gift of any being
is that it exists. Born 50 years after Newton's death,
Carl Gauss was familiar with the angular

defect. He lived on its outsized surfaces. His beloved died
in childbirth with their newborn son, and soon after a bereft
daughter followed. Staring through his theorems, through
fearsome curves of elliptical space, he saw only the back

of his head. Random errors like a bell around a mean.
Believe me, my dear friend, he wrote, *tragedy has woven itself
through my life like a red ribbon.* He wrote:
Even the bright sky makes me sadder. All work is secret,

Karen Solie

all times unreasonable. To love is to consent to distance.
I went back, to the dirt track through the Ravenscrag
Formation, its rose striations in cuts and erosions,
greasewood, sage and cactus prevailing on the upslope,

willow, cottonwood close to water, long bonebeds
of the Cretaceous and Paleocene, graves we worship
by digging at. I walked the margins of the Williston Basin
without knowing it; over sandstones, shale, muddy siltstone,

claystones, lateral sheets of braided river gravels, near lost
on the lignite alluvial plain within sight of uranium deposits
JNR Corp. has its eye on, and probably trespassing. Some people
are outfitted with odd and foolish habits. An unregulated

look. Has the devil any servant on earth so perfect
as the stranger? Who hears, always, dice thrown
on the outskirts, and whose cause is yet to be proven?
Things aren't meant to happen, yet they happen

nonetheless. I stayed in that country, travelled until dark
the first night of the Perseids while cloud massed
to the discernible horizon, and read it as a sign,
though it was no sign. Your leaving opened up a view

Postscript

like that from the cliffs in their coarse conglomerate
sequence, out to where lines, the great circles, intersect.
Where symmetries radiate from a first principle and all opposites
are contained, no one thing taking precedence. That day,

the smell of rained-on grasses was narcotic, rising
from the ground in a mineral swarm. It was added to us,
our fire visible for miles, as late afternoon bent
to the rangeland and laid its shining weapons down.

NICK THRAN

Aria with a Mirror and No Earplugs

It is spring inside the industrial dryer,
where a mess of towels bloom
as a single carnation, whose petals
will cover the water-slick bodies
of swimmers up from the pool.
It is spring over the porcelain bowl
between two people dining
at their local dive. The endless talk,
the shrimp wonton she holds aloft
while describing her childhood springs
in the Ozarks, or some lush place you imagine
Waits is reaching for in his gravel-dust bawler:
You Can Never Hold Back Spring.

"You can never hold back spring,"
not the runoff, not the brand new smells
in the street-car, which are only the old smells
of last spring returning, as real as sweat,
as the inward made public, as the squeak
of a box-spring mattress upstairs where neighbours swear
at each other in the urgent, new tongue of the season:
You gorgeous cunt. You dirty little spring . . .

CAREY TOANE

Seventy-two-hour emergency

1

In the dark, I feed him peanut butter and honey
from my fingers, bargain for chunks of granola
bar, ponder dried legumes and what we were thinking.
What water to soak? To boil? Rumi's lentil sits hard
and we are meting our three litres each, per day. In
the mornings I study the bagman's alphabet and when
he is hungry, my heart is a souk selling maple syrup
and rose petals dusted in turmeric. We crank
the radio in unison. We stop flushing the toilet, stop
talking about it. Sure of rescue, we build primitive statues
out of signal flares and duct tape. We push down the cork
on that bottle of wine, finally. We regard outsiders with
suspicion. We keep our own chaos.

2

There is no other word for Ziploc. In emergencies,
you can use disposable plates and forks and not feel guilty.
Everything else requires batteries. All those years
you never bought a utility knife and never thought about it.
If you had a safety deposit box, you could crawl in there
with your original documents and lock the door behind you.
Swallow the key. She never learned to sew, to make
bread, and it doesn't matter because the oven's still
off. The candlelight is romantic, although the canned food
gave you gas and there's no hiding it. If only you'd

taken those dance lessons together, found the time, if only
you could remember how to play Euchre, if only you could
look it up online and settle this Ziploc issue, once and for all.

3

If you want the broadest possible protection for your home
and personal belongings, press one. If you want to protect
your home against most unexpected situations, press two.
To protect your home against a limited number of disasters,
including fire, lightning, windstorm and hail, press three.
Now, cover your detached structures. Cover the upgrades
to your unit. Cover your lawn, trees, plants, shrubs. Cover
your non-owned property. Cover your money, coins
and bullion. Cover your gold-, silver- and pewterware.
Cover watercraft and watercraft motors. Cover your pets
and furs, your manuscripts, stamps and counterfeit. Cover
your guns and ammunition, up to one thousand dollars.
Cover your freezer, no limit. Cover lock and key.

ANNE-MARIE TURZA

Anthem for a Small Country

In my country we admire the ambitious dust: long into the night,
for endless hours, it practises such gentleness on the window's sill.

Our country's flower is the rose in the curved bed of the fingernail.
In the cloud's menagerie, our animal is the solitary wisp.

As for religion, we peer into drains and the old burrows
of earthworms, looking for the shyness of our shrinking god.

Our territory often dwindles to a smooth slip
of a pillow, a fleece blanket and the bed's four posts.

What we lack in fellow citizens, we address by mumbling
to ourselves. And to the white cat, and the calico.

From the industry of sleep, exporting
small, domestic sounds.

PAUL TYLER

Manitoba Maples

Beaning from pavement moss, eyelets in walls,
      green-quivered delicates spiked into asphalt morass,
helpless, twig-legged. Until their roots python,
      bulge into sewer veins, godzilla-limbs arching
over rooftops, opportunistic cuckoo trees, seeding
      fund-pinched, zoned-to-be-condoized intersections.
Unnoticed in dumpster-moist darkness, and sprayed
      brick lairs, casually sprouting, these halloween
decorations gone feral loiter in disused lots plotting chaos.
      Megalomaniac weeds, bug havens, bird bramble,
messed-up, misshapen bouffant heavies—more names
      than a nineteenth century countess. No one just says:
tree. Laid-back neighbours suddenly insist on shredders,
      buy mid-life crisis chain saws. One maple
rumoured to have dropped a branch on a widow's head
      as if waiting years for the right angle. Another
slipped its muddy claw inside a basement duct,
      opened the house right up in a hemophilic spilling
of oil and heartache. Near a stumbling Manitoba town
      I saw some last-century hutch stabbed up
the middle by a young maple—pronged out windows,
      a deciduous mess of bankruptcy.
Could be your life next, the neighbour points,
      eyeing up the grand trunk's indifference
to fence lines—could cause wires to snap, flatten your roses,
      a cat, might bring down satellite beams, screw

with phone calls to old world aunts, nest in the driveway's
        winter heaves, spring through the convalescent Camaro
on blocks, stripping it to its chassis. Your foundation next—
        see that crack—it'll creep inside while you sleep,
drop its pods in your dreams, this shambling mound of leaves,
        pollen puffing lawn-squid; it has nothing better to do.

PATRICK WARNER

The Mole

As though a hand had reached inside to rub
my liver. This was the nose of the mole.

Later, I felt a prickle, a draught in my eye.
This was the southwest breeze blowing
where the stone-blind mole had passed.

This was the meat of what was unspoken.
The absolute bedrock of morals, the top-soil
of incomprehension in which you turned
and said: Your wife tells me everything.

This was the unknown known, the mole
surfacing through the green. And blinking
by the swings on that suburban lawn
was my penchant for darkness and filth,
my penchant for sticking my nose in.

ZACHARIAH WELLS

To the Superb Lyrebird,
that Cover Band of the Australian Bush

Mountebank dancer and manic mimic,
Is there a bush ruckus your syrinx can't clone?
Bubbly corkpops and glassclinks at picnics;
Kookaburra's cackle when its cover is blown;
Alarm panic, siren wail, chainsaw drone;
Motor drive's whirr and black aperture's click
As it captures your likeness; trigger-snick
And barrel blast of the shot that missed home;
Honey-eaters' chitter and moth-wings' flutter;
The barking of dogs and the crying of babies;
The lunatic howl of a dingo with rabies;
Wind-bang stutter of a torn-loose shutter;
All the ring tones of a cellular phone—
No song you can't sing, but no song your own.

PATRICIA YOUNG

Night-Running

> *Trial-marriages . . . [allow] the young couple to spend the night together*
> *. . . Night-courtship flourishes in stable and well-knit European*
> *communities not liable to disorganization by contact with strangers.*
> —Havelock Ellis, *Studies in the Psychology of Sex*

Tarrying, the Irish called it, *hand-fasting, bundling.*
In Holland they *quested*. The Norwegians
said *night-running*, and no wonder, the great distances
between them, the boy loping

across his father's fields, plunging into the dank
pine forest, flowering lingonberry and tysbast, whiskey
rags streaking the sky, he's running out to the western
edge, grass slapping his ankles, kittiwakes and whooper swans,
the blood in his head bright as the sun that will not
go down. The girl hangs out her bedroom
window. Last Sunday during church

hymns he turned and looked straight
at her. *O Jesus, Sweet and Lowly,* his look was a hot
summer wind that blew her wide open. He's still miles away
but she can feel the earth's tremor, his feet pounding
closer, his body springing towards hers,
and then
                    a shadowy figure in silver light
                                        he emerges
from the clump of trees beside the new barn,
            now slowing   breathing hard   circling the woodpile.

94

He kicks a stone as though he just
happened by and is that her
moving behind the curtains?

A ladder leans against the house.
He climbs and enters, stands before her,
an awkward offering. *Now what?* his tongue-tied
hands ask. If her heart's beating madly he does not
hear it, if she throws back the quilt he'll take off
his boots, but what else can he take
off, the rules are the rules.
                    Who are they,

this girl sitting upright against the pillows,
prim as a matron about to serve tea, this boy
whose hair smells of wind and grilled dogfish.

Sweat runs down his back and he tells her he's warm
running so far, would she mind if he took off his
shirt, well, she's warm too, this heavy
skirt, these woollen leggings! They're young,
shy, turn away from
each other to unbutton
and remove,
turn
     and turn back

Patricia Young

newly born
skin
rucked over bone, but still they don't
touch, they lie side by side on her straw tick mattress,
listening to the timbers settle and creak, silence
so huge it swells up to the rafters and breaks

into talk. For hours they talk
nonsense in her high narrow bed, until her father's
boots clomp past the door, down the stairs and out to the woodshed.

Crack of the axe blade, dry clatter of kindling
as their talk leads into next week, next
month, bonfires and feasting,
schnapps and maypoles, and *Who will you dance with?*
she asks, her thigh brushing
                    his thigh,
          an accident
to which there's no answer, there's nothing more
to say now the world's become
thigh, now *thigh*
                    is the only word
they know: a night road lit up by candles,
garden of sweet mosses, dull hum
vibrating against the roof of their skulls.

DAVID ZIEROTH

How Brave

. . . make a complete exit from life, not in anger, but simply, freely,
with integrity, making this leaving of it at least one achievement in
your life.
—Marcus Aurelius, *Meditations*

How brave of a worldly one dying
on his white antiseptic bed to say
there is no god and I have become death
his last breath a final simple heaving
not extending upwards into arms
of waiting deities, his forehead damp
not with excitement or exaltation
but effort of animal exertion that must
be borne, yes, and thus he suffers
the magnitude of the task, of leaving
corporeal substance, the scrabbling hand
and even what's called consciousness
the flame that asks always why *is*
feels both unborn and deathless

How bravely those who cannot believe
meet the moment when an afterlife
begins for others, not them, and how
they stay stoic, having learned ways
not to hope or despair—denying either—
but to penetrate the mystery of the day
in mornings when they live clear headed

David Zieroth

—in afternoons they sag, work-logged—
in evenings when they stop to weigh
the stars, imagining not so much
themselves arriving as dust from such
a distance, nor being small beyond
meaning itself—just breathing hearts
beating numbers, recognizing time

How brave to die when we can't behold
our parents arriving to greet our souls
embarking apparently from pale beds where
we fight for the dignity of our aloneness
though clustered around by attendant
machines and our bewildered children
How we have raged for our right not to be
herded by churchy cherubs, not to further
cosmic harmonics in our progression from
matter toward what can hardly be said
To enter rot and raise no arm and shout!
To prepare our gratitude and give back
without benefit of flood or inferno, wordlessly
what we borrowed in our mothers' wombs

JAN ZWICKY

Autobiography

In the years when winter snow piled up
along the edges of the streets, beneath the windows,
on the lee side of the hedge,
I did my homework at a desk my father built,
set in the corner of my bedroom, facing west.
Which was my choice, I think. The second desk,
I know it was. And once I moved out, the apartments
with the bad floors and the crazy plumbing,
the wallpaper I was always steaming off, I'd take
the place because it had a workspace
that did not face east.

Those cold bright years.
How long I spent, trying to die.

Such injustice. When every morning
it's spring again. Every morning
the light melts the snow—
before books, before desks, before windows,
before pain, before amazement.

POEM NOTES & COMMENTARIES

Ken Babstock, *"Lee Atwater in Blowing Snow"*

Atwater is often named as the savant-ish ground-level inventor of neo-con dissembling, eff-the-facts, saying-it-makes-it-true type political strategy as we know it today. He was a mean operator. His biography is truly Shakespearean; sunglasses, blues-rock, parties, the late eighties, then ending his days with a brain tumour, virtually friendless, confined to a wheelchair, entertaining visits from religious advisers of all stripes.

Coleridge was an early reader of German Idealism, Kant, etc., and my crass understanding of the story since then is one of Western Thought pointing out the disenchanting fact that saying it does not in fact make it so. Plus I've always loved mildly severe weather. I remember, as a boy, falling asleep one evening in a snow bank on the grounds of a darkened United Church, during a storm—because it was comfy. *Gesuglichkeit.*

John Barton, *"Mill Creek Reverdie"*

A reverdie, according to Robin Skelton in *The Shapes of Our Singing*, his posthumous encyclopedia of verse forms from around the world, is a French poem celebrating spring and composed to be a dance. Each of its five or six quatrains has ten-syllable lines, with the line endings linked together by assonance or full rhyme (AAAA, BBBB, etc.). I've varied this footprint slightly by breaking the quatrains into couplets, with staggered indentions to introduce additional light and breath—perhaps the sudden and painful breath and light of the long longed-for northern spring, or, in the spirit of the dance, a more nimble sure-*foot*edness to animate my metre. Mill Creek Ravine ("reverdie" for my purposes of course being a riff on "ravine") runs into the North Saskatchewan River valley in Edmonton immediately below Faculté Saint-Jean, where I studied French (and Gide) in the late 1970s. The spring fevers I hope to evoke catch my two protagonists at variance with one another. Their dance is one of counterpoint. The expansive steps of one lead him to an anointed fecundity; the steps of the other tend him instead towards an unrequited, if fruitful fruitlessness.

Anne Compton, "Heat in April"

"Heat in April," an amorphic sonnet, explores the experience of bereavement in the midst of spring's lush flowering.

Allan Cooper, "Two Glimpses"

The prose poem as a form goes back nearly 200 years. The French poet Aloysius Bertrand (1807-1841), who influenced both Baudelaire and Mallarmé, is one of the acknowledged fathers of the form. I have always been drawn to the ecologically-minded Romantics, including John Clare, who wrote clear prose poems about a robin, snakes, a landrail, the bark of trees, and a nightingale around the time of Bertrand. Clare's "Pleasant Sounds" (*I Am: The Selected Poetry of John Clare*, Farrar, Straus and Giroux, 2003) ends with a wonderful image: "The flirt of the groundlark's wing from the stubbles, how sweet such pictures on dewy mornings when the dew flashes from its brown feathers."

Henry David Thoreau, another practitioner of the form, wrote literally dozens of prose poems in the *Journals* about such natural objects as herons, small streams, a turtle's shell, and a rooster. One thing that distinguishes the prose poem from a lyric poem is the amount of detail it absorbs. Rather than being a straight scientific description, the rhythm of the prose poem modulates; it carries the same music and imagery we expect from good lyric poetry.

There are literally dozens of contemporary prose poets, but two masters of the form are the late French poet Francis Ponge and the eminent American poet Robert Bly. I began writing prose poems in the late 1970s, encouraged by their work. I was attracted to the way the form absorbed specific details from the subject I was writing about, whether that subject was a porcupine, an oak desk, or my daughter. With prose poems, there's always the challenge of how much detail to include, and how much to leave out.

There is an old Chinese saying: "When a question is posed ceremoniously, the universe listens." A question is present in each prose poem, although often this question is not overt. We could call it the shadow behind the written words. Basho, the great Japanese haiku poet, gave much attention to the natural world. In this poem, we can feel a shadow behind the morning glories:

> These morning glories—
> are they my friends
> or not.

To me this poem is a question, not a quandary. The poem is particularly poignant now, as we face a worldwide ecological crisis.

Basho also knew that once men and women understand that they are as much a part of the natural world as a grass blade, marvellous things happen. In this haiku, Basho is talking about himself as much as he is about the bee:

> The bee leaves
> the deep flower
> reluctantly.

When I began "Two Glimpses," one challenge I set for myself was to see how much detail I could leave out and still create a successful prose poem. I had caught only fleeting glances of the porcupine and the toad, so I had to write swiftly about the subjects at hand. In this case I used the brevity of Basho's elegant haiku as my model.

Mary Dalton, "Three Centos"

These variations on the ancient cento (a compilation of lines from one author as a form of tribute) are part of a much longer series. They raise questions about the nature of subjectivity, originality, quotation, tonality, musicality. Various seemingly contradictory sets of impulses are at play in the work.

I came to this particular form of collage before I knew of the existence of the cento of tradition. I invented it to meet the needs of a specific piece I was working on. I then discovered that it allowed me to address a number of questions about the making of poetry.

The lines that make up "Cloth" are taken from the seventh lines of the following poems, in the order given:
Talvikki Ansel, "Xylem"
Daniel Hall, "After Reading"
Kevin Craft, "Birches"
Alfred, Lord Tennyson, "The time draws near the birth of Christ"
Stanley Plumly, "The Morning America Changed"
Lola Haskins, "Prayer for the Everglades"
Cecilia Woloch, "Why I Believed, As a Child, That People Had Sex in Bathrooms"
Marilyn Kallet, "Circe, Did You?"
Richard Wilbur, "Some Words Inside of Words"
Priscila Uppal, "Three Cats Guard This House"
Rachel Hadas, "The Avenue"
Phillis Levin, "May Day"
Cornelius Eady, "Handymen"
Tobias Hill, "A Year in London (November)"
Martha Collins, "Sheer, If We Could Be"
Mark Jarman, "Reminder"
Molly Peacock, "The Blush"
Susan Stewart, "The Owl"

The lines that appear in "A Little Tin Pail" are taken from the fifth lines of the following poems, in the order given:
Robert Bly, "Listening to the Köln Concert"
William Carlos Williams, "Smell"
Michael Blumenthal, "A Man Lost by a River"
Miguel Hernandez, "War," trans. Hardie St. Martin
Rainer Maria Rilke, "Sometimes A Man Stands Up During Supper," trans. Robert Bly
Federico García Lorca, "Rundown Church (Ballad of the First World War)," trans. Robert Bly
Louis Simpson, "Big Dream, Little Dream"
Rainer Maria Rilke, "Sonnets to Orpheus VIII," trans. Robert Bly
William Jay Smith, "American Primitive"
Mary Oliver, "Blue Iris"
Kerry Hardie, "Dublin Train, Solstice"
Ezra Pound, "Canto LXXXI"
Katha Pollitt, "Onion"
Ann Egan, "Lyre Blackbird"
Stanley Kunitz, "The Portrait"
Robert Mezey, "A Thousand Chinese Dinners"
Anna Akhmatova, "Twenty-First. Night. Monday," trans. Jane Kenyan
David Ignatow, "A First on TV"
Ann Egan, "Kind in Sounds"
Kerry Hardie, "Le Cheval," from "Sunflowers"
Louis Simpson, "American Poetry"
Robert Bly, "Passing An Orchard By Train"
Charles Simic, "Breasts"
Harry Martinson, "The Earthworm," trans. Robert Bly

The lines that appear in "Automatic Doors" are taken from the seventh
lines of the following poems:
Simon Armitage, "Not the Furniture Game"
Simon Armitage, "Parable of the Dead Donkey"
Simon Armitage, "Dream Holiday"
Fleur Adcock, "Happy Ending"
Fleur Adcock, "Accidental"
Don Paterson, "Sunset, Visingsö"
Don Paterson, "The Ferryman's Arms"
W.H. Auden, "Heavy Date"
Don Paterson, "The Trans-Siberian Express"
Elizabeth Bishop, "Songs for a Coloured Singer"
Richard Wilbur, "Orchard Trees, January"
H.D., "Heat"
Herménégilde Chiasson, *Beatitudes*
Elizabeth Bishop, "It Is Marvellous"
John Betjeman, "Myfanwy"

Barry Dempster, "Mary Lake Writing Retreat"
Mary Lake, near Huntsville, a couple of hours north of Toronto, was the
perfect place for an October writers' retreat. We did the usual prompts,
first drafts and Poets' Walks through the forest. I remember one of my
friends immersing her face in the rapids to see what the agitation felt like,
another standing beside a tall maple, trying to put into words the ticking
sound that seemed to be coming from deep inside the tree. I came across
a clearing strewn with red, orange, and yellow leaves and spent twenty
minutes struggling with description, each new attempt less resonant than
the one before. Sure, it's a poet's job to learn the world, to recognize and
celebrate, to give voice to all the beauty and tragedy around us. But to en-
gage with experience through the medium of pen and paper can be like

wrapping yourself in plastic, not letting the wind or the rain actually touch your skin. We had a grand time of it, learning to keep our note-books in our pockets until after the goose bumps were gone.

Kildare Dobbs, "It"

The subject of this poem is something we don't like to think about. The vision "It" expresses appeared in the real world to me when I was half dreaming.

Don Domanski, "Gloria Mundi"

The poem was written in response to a friend's loss of a family member, her resulting sorrow and lack of sleep. It was meant as a lullaby, a soothing of heart and nerves.

Glen Downie, "Nocturnal Visitors"

The pest removal vans are coming for them, because they've knocked over our compost bins once too often. Meanwhile we're spilling thousands of gallons of oil a day into the ocean. Is somebody coming for us?

Sue Goyette, "This Last Lamp"

I was thinking about darkness when I wrote "This Last Lamp." Literal darkness and how, unless you're in a very rural setting, it's becoming harder to find. I went driving one night looking for it outside Halifax and was amazed at how many security lights snapped on every time I thought I finally found it. This elusive darkness became a rich metaphor and represented, for me, the border between all kinds of wilderness, what we've domesticated and how far we'll go.

Rosemary Griebel, "Wonder"

For a number of years I had a job that involved regular visits to "God's waiting rooms"—seniors' lodges and care centres. While there are some happy memories, more often I had an overwhelming sense of human tragedy, resignation, and abandonment. Each time I left one of the facilities it was like closing a door to a neglected library filled with great history and wisdom.

In writing this poem, the end-stopped line was a very deliberate element.

Adrienne Gruber, "The Rope"

On January 10, 2007 at around 1:30 p.m., I left work during a record-breaking snowstorm in Saskatoon. I trudged in heavy drifts to my car and watched through the gusts of wind as businesses shut down and abandoned cars littered the streets. On the drive home (took almost two hours) I couldn't see the headlights of the car in front of me, much less the buildings I was driving past. Streetlights were useless. I was struggling personally during this time. Experiencing that storm yanked me out of that struggle, thrusting me into a new world filled with a different kind of chaos.

This poem is about trying to get home. Not home in the obvious sense of the word, but home as a feeling, a belonging. It's about keeping one's grip on reality, on the things that ground you. The event this poem is based on reflects what poems actually *do*, how they function. They pull us swiftly and expertly into new worlds, into uncharted territory, and in the midst of that transition, they transform us.

Jamella Hagen, "Driving Daytona"

This poem came out of stalled work on another project: by accident, through a side door, like most things. The "you" in the poem isn't imperative to me, it's more a form of distancing, the way we often use the past tense to add politeness or a sense of the unreal to something that is actually present or future, as in "Would it be all right if I opened the window?" or "Had we but world enough and time . . ." Maybe that's what I was looking for: a grammar of ambivalence. That or a race car, I guess.

Steven Heighton, "Some Other Just Ones"

"Some Other Just Ones" is a response to Jorge Luis Borges's poem "The Just" ("*El Justo*"). The italicized first and last lines that frame my poem are translated from the Spanish of Borges's original; the rest is my own simple litany or catalogue of those people who, in small ways, redeem the day. I don't usually write "from life," not without radical transformation, but, in this case, most of my lines are based on real people, people living here in Kingston. I don't usually write list-poems, either, because when I do I tend to get sloppy, plausibly fluent, lazily capacious—all dangers endemic to the form. But I loved the Borges original and I'd been writing some harsh judgmental poems and I craved a furlough from indignation. I wanted to sing about my neighbours and the people I know—even the ones I dislike in some ways, since they too are saviours of something.

In the same way that it's easier to maintain grievance than gratitude, it seems easier for most poets to write "negative" stuff (sad, angry, grieving) than "positive." Certainly that's been true in my own case. But my experience of writing, publishing, and performing "Some Other Just Ones" has been so, yes, positive that I know I'll try writing this way again.

Warren Heiti, "The Day"

At sunset, the Danforth's corridor can channel the light (not unlike the Trinity College Chapel), and as I stood at the corner, transfixed, the whole day came rushing over the viaduct and focused itself in those apples; and I turned from them, and walked into the west, and the crowd, their faces indescribably beautiful, seemed to be surging out of the sun. Beautiful—but the word is feeble, even embarrassing, it cannot carry the experience.—What is the experience?—Perhaps no one has articulated it more forcefully than Rilke in his "Archaic Torso of Apollo," or Alkibiades in Plato's *Symposium*: it is like seeing something that sees right through you; and, being seen, you are, suddenly, ashamed at the shape of your life; you need, urgently, to change.—Why?—The question eventually leads either to scepticism or to theory; better, I guess, to trust the testimonies, and our own experiences. Plato himself, impressed by the phenomenology of beauty and impelled by the fiercest desire for clarity, has the courage to submit his theory to the challenge of Parmenides. Through the mask of Sokrates, Plato asks, "What if an idea"—such as beauty, itself by itself with itself—"is like the day? Can't that be in many places at once without breaking apart?" And through the mask of Parmenides, he performs a shell game with the metaphor: "Charming. Don't you mean like a sail, spread over many people?" Sokrates reluctantly takes the bait, and thus betrays the Platonic metaphysics to the paper shredder; but perched at that fork in the conversation, we are invited to think about his forsaken image. (I am grateful to Jan Zwicky for having amplified Plato's questions.)

M.G.R. Hickman-Barr, "Cattle Egret"
For me as a poet, everything in poetic language is the wilderness—an otherness in consciousness to be encountered again and again. In this poem, I chose to re-name and poetically recover the text of a great love. This exploration parallels that of an incessant reader helpless against the compulsion to read even a shred of paper, torn from the whole.

Maureen Hynes, "The Last Cigarette"
"The Last Cigarette" is a both a marker and an invocation as I renounced an addiction. I'd planned to quit smoking before I took a kayaking trip off Haida Gwaii (Queen Charlotte Islands), and I'd also immersed myself in the art, culture, and legends of the Haida. Just before the kayaking trip,

I drove myself up to Massett for a ceremonial moment in the north island
to smoke the last few cigarettes in my pack. If I could paint the moment,
it would be in shades of grey. I hope the poem captures those greys, my
fear and panic and deluded clinging to the sensuality of smoking, and my
plea to all the Haida spirits who'd given and endured so much—and the
bracing coldness of the surf to restore health and sanity.

Michael Johnson, "In Praise of the Village Idiot"

This piece came my first month writing in college, when I didn't know yet
how rarely some poems come in just this way, almost whole, like a gift.
From my boyhood came this old man who roamed the campus in Lu-
kanga, Zaïre, where my parents were missionaries. He was touched, and
loved to jangle this small band of bells like the saddest tambourine. So I
put them around his ankle and started with the title and the line "Did I
make music today?," which I'd read somewhere and gladly stolen. I never
knew his name, but his hair was mesmeric and lumpish from whatever
side he'd slept on, flecked with grass like gilt in the sun. He was certain of
his own beauty, the way some days he strutted and ignored us. I envy the
music in his head that paced him, that accompanied his long, sad solos—
that let him walk, every day, as in the garden of God's smile.

Jim Johnstone, "Disgraceland"

"Disgraceland" began for me with a name, and proceeded to evolve into
a poem based on a speech delivered by Orson Welles on the Wiener
Riesenrad Ferris wheel at the conclusion of Carol Reed's 1949 film noir,
The Third Man. Referring to the residents of Vienna below as dots, Welles
notes: "In Italy, for thirty years under the Borgias they had warfare, terror,
murder, and bloodshed—but they produced Michelangelo, Leonardo
da Vinci, and the Renaissance. In Switzerland they had brotherly love,
they had five hundred years of democracy and peace, and what did that

produce? The cuckoo clock." There are several historical inaccuracies in this snippet of dialogue, and "Disgraceland" is based on untruths of a similar variety.

Sonnet L'Abbé, "The Trees Have Loved Us All Along"

My obsession for the past three years has been to feel out why we use plant metaphors to talk about three things: language (root words), our nervous and neurological systems (dendrites, stem cells and brain stems, seminal ideas), and organizational structures (bank branches, decision trees). Spiritual growth as a biological something? Joy as a kind of photosynthesis? Sometimes my pursuit seems a little crazy, like hunting for a cure to a sickness we haven't discovered yet. I wonder, why do I care so much about how we are like plants? Then I go out and notice a tree. I am struck again by something central, something elemental and balanced. My body relaxes, my breath slows. There is movement at the centre of rings of pith and through the spinal column. That trunk there—is *alive*. My mindbody tries to organize that perception into words. Sex is somewhere at the heart of it.

Fiona Tinwei Lam, "Aquarium"

When my son was an infant and toddler, I wrote a sequence of poems set in ordinary places that detailed the journey into single parenthood. (Many of these poems were included in my recent book, *Enter the Chrysanthemum*.) There can be precise and lucid moments where the symbolic potential within even the most mundane of activities is revealed. This poem about loss juxtaposes tone and style to both mirror and frame its content. The poem moves from inside to outside, ideal to real, protected to exposed, whole to incomplete, with the middle stanza bridging the two poles. The intensity and intimacy of the poem are linked to its apparent simplicity.

Evelyn Lau, "Swimming Lessons"
This was my first trip to Hawaii, and I was surprised by the suddenness of the sunsets (in the poem, this is mirrored by how one's mood can shift in an instant when something hurtful is said), and the strength of the sea's undertow. A dip in the ocean became more than I bargained for. What struck me afterwards was how I'd previously romanticized the moments before possible death, believing I would have time to rummage through memories, regrets, etc. Instead it all came down to the need to breathe; everything else was wiped away. Incidentally, I am still in mourning for the designer sunglasses, which are no doubt floating somewhere in the Pacific Garbage Patch. Or maybe a very cool fish is wearing them . . .

Katherine Lawrence, "Dear—"
I imagined a conversation with Mary Pratt, one of Canada's most eminent artists, after seeing a retrospective exhibition of her work at the MacKenzie Art Gallery in Regina. I felt as though the subjects of her oil paintings—jars of jelly, poppyseed cake, a wedding dress—were both numinous and erotic. These qualities are known well to those who study Mary Pratt's work, but I wondered if a poetic dialogue might bring a deeper attentiveness to the way ordinary objects can assume the role of witness in our lives.

Ross Leckie, "The Critique of Pure Reason"
Critique of Pure Reason is a large book by the German philosopher Immanuel Kant, first published in 1781. He argues, as I understand it, that our senses are already organizing and arranging what we perceive before the mind's analytical abilities can put perception into categories. I think metaphor shapes everything we see the moment we see it, and poetry is the purest expression of metaphor, so poetry literally teaches us how to see. How much does reason have to do with what we see? Not much, I

suspect. I went for a walk in northern British Columbia and I wanted a simple, reasonable explanation for the strange world I was witnessing, but I couldn't find it, so I consoled myself with arithmetic. And I had my walking friends Donna Kane, George Sipos, and Jan Zwicky.

Tim Lilburn, "Rupert's Land"

Rupert's Land was the name given by the Hudson's Bay Company to the land it managed and traded into from 1670 to 1869, roughly all the territory drained by rivers emptying into Hudson Bay. This land, together with the old Northwest Territory, the HBC somehow sold to Canada, making the company and its shareholders even richer. This poem makes a present day return to this terrain and to the idea of Rupert's Land. It's part of a manuscript called *Assiniboia*.

Dave Margoshes, "The Chicken Coop"

I frequently mine my own life for poems, as most poets do. Often the "autobiography" is as much fiction as it is fact. "The Chicken Coop" is as close to real autobiography as any of my poems—it's an enduring part of the mythology of my family, but there really was a converted chicken coop, a lost house, an old farm, the glass of port in my father's hand, his regret. On the other hand, I was an infant when we lived in the coop, so the poem is based on family lore, not true memory.

Jim Nason, "Black Ice"

I was born in December, the year the movie *It's a Wonderful Life* was released. My parents loved the movie and named me after James Stewart. A few days before writing this poem I was ill, symptoms included nausea and vertigo. The experience frightened the hell out of me—in a flu-induced delirium, I dragged myself off the bedroom floor and wrote "Black Ice." It was originally titled "Vertigo."

114

Catherine Owen, "White Sale"

In 2005, the entire Ayles Ice Shelf on Ellesmere Island, a topographical presence some 3,500 years old, came smashing down in an hour of overly warm temperatures and brisk winds. Once a monstrous outcropping more than 1,500 football fields in length, it is now a shrinking continent of ice, its unique geography annulled. This historic descent was an impetus to imagining a world in which the cold, among other species of being, is becoming extinct, another rare commodity for sale as it vanishes. "White Sale" also sprang from the sight of one of Edmontonian multimedia artist's Sydney Lancaster's encaustic pieces, a canvas of wax into which was embedded seeds and feathers and skulls, providing my mind with a rich and abstract terrain on which to wander.

P.K. Page, "Cullen in Old Age"

Zailig Pollock, P.K. Page's literary executor, says of her "Cullen" poems: "It is tempting to identify the protagonist . . . as a fictional self-portrait, if only because Cullen ages in parallel with the author, and shares many of her experiences. But perhaps it would make more sense to see Cullen as a fictional, and not uncritical, portrait of a fellow pilgrim through the journey."

Rebecca Leah Păpucaru, "Rosalind Franklin in Open-Toe Sandals"

Frumpy Jewish intellectual woman. The photo James Watson had chosen of pioneering Anglo-Jewish scientist Rosalind Franklin confirmed this. Admittedly, not a flattering photo. Even her lipstick looked aggressive. When Watson wrote his memoir, high on his Nobel Prize, Rosalind Franklin was unable to defend herself, having died of ovarian cancer. Did the non-Jewish students in my undergraduate English course (Intro duction to Narrative) accept Watson's portrayal of an asexual, irrational harridan who deserved to have her pioneering X-rays of the double helix stolen? To Watson, Franklin and her lousy haircut were impediments to a glorious new age of scientific progress. As a Jewish woman and scholar, I could not bear that photo, never forgot it. Then I read Brenda Maddox's biography. With photos! In her Dior outfits, Franklin looked as chic as Coco Chanel. Not that it mattered. Not that it ever should have mattered. But the race to discover the blueprint of humanity boiled down, in the end, to a photo finish.

Marilyn Gear Pilling, "Billy Collins Interviewed On Stage at Chautauqua"

Both as writer and human being —yes, I see them as almost two different entities—I enjoy the confluence of acute seeing, self-deprecatory humour, and wisdom that happens "often enough" in Billy Collins's poems, as in "Dharma": "if only I were not her god." But Billy Collins did not seem comfortable that morning on stage at Chautauqua, and he applied a number of rules to all poets that seemed to me to apply only to his own process and his own poems. That afternoon, as I sat in the centre of Chautauqua, an idyllic-seeming place, thinking about Don McKay's words, "One cannot live in the sublime," I got that frisson up the backbone that for me heralds a poem. Lines that I regard as gently skewering the morning's interview arose in my head. I hastened to record them on the only paper I had at hand: the flyleaf of "The Trouble with Poetry."

Lenore & Beth Rowntree, "7lbs. 6oz."

Two sisters—the similarities are many, the differences few. This poem explores the subtle things that determine who gets a gentle ride in life and who gets a rough one. Many aspects of the poem are found. Emotions found in Lenore's memory, triggered by poems found in Beth's wastebasket, purse, desk, and dresser.

Armand Garnet Ruffo, "The Tap is Dripping Memory"
In traditional Anishinaabe (Ojibway) culture it's said that we have two souls or spirits. One that is with us during our waking lives, and one that is with us during our sleeping lives. Because I'm currently working on a project about the acclaimed Anishinaabe painter Norval Morrisseau, whose sense of spirituality is at the centre of his work, I have been thinking a lot about the connection between our inner and outer lives. Am I dreaming or remembering these things? How does the inner dream world inform and shape the outer experiential world? This poem does not try to answer these or any other questions but rather explores the concept by bringing together disparate events at the spirit level.

Lori Saint-Martin, "Quatre fruits/Four Fruits"
Some—not all—of the four fragments of this poetic suite are autobiographical. They seem very sad and resigned now, and I suppose that captures a way of loving I once experienced. They are little elegies, moments of longing strung together by the idea of intimacy (or the illusion of it). The fruits, like a desire just out of reach, a vision that slips by the corner of the eye, seem to me now to be the real heart of the matter.

Peter Sanger, "Sea Horse (for M.)"
"Sea Horse" is one of a series of birthday poems written for my wife. It was accompanied by the gift of a life-sized sea horse, carved from Waterford lead crystal. At one level, the poem concerns a particular marriage; at another, the relationship between poetry and love, art and civilization (and whatever human possibilities destroy both love and civilization). The poem celebrates the sea horse's existence (and poetry's) as a small, mimetic playfulness and as a joyous, unpredictable, individual, intelligent response to what might otherwise seem biological determinism. The poem begins with the discrimination of

a word. Perhaps that is the sea horse's version of Genesis. Perhaps the mind might sing.

Robyn Sarah, "Messenger"

I'm a regular walker on Mount Royal (that oversized pebble in the middle of Montreal to which the name "mountain" has clung), and like many Montrealers I tend to go straight from boots into sandals in the spring. The serpentine road to the lookout, shared by walkers and cyclists, is a dirt-and-cinder one; bicycle wheels send the fine gravel flying. My poems tend to speak for themselves, but the title of this one is telling: I'm the sort of person who sees messages in things. The proverbial stone in the shoe calls attention to itself in a way that's hard to ignore, yet we seem to have a curious tolerance for it. In this poem, I started out looking for what the stone might be telling me, but ended in the recognition that my own willingness to accommodate it was telling, too. "Harry my sole" isn't so far from "Harrow my soul."

Eleonore Schönmaier, "Weightless"

Canoeing and minimalism: both preserve a stillness that reverberates beyond maps and pages.

David Seymour, "The Photo Double"

About five years ago I spent six months in Mexico working as a photo double for the lead actor in a feature film of no small budget or ambitions. Each morning at dawn I would don the period wardrobe, strap on sword and sheath, accustom myself once again to his gait and bearing, then wander the studio waiting for a call to set when he would be busy elsewhere filming something dialogue-bound in extreme close-up. The concept of identity becomes manifold in a situation whose purpose is the fabrication of the real. My job was to mimic an actor whose job it was to play out the role of a fictional character who in turn was based on a composite of several actual historical figures. And here the writer steps in with yet another mimetic mode, a poem focusing on simulacra. The Aristotelian *is/is not* formula for metaphor notwithstanding, I became for this *enfant terrible* a kind of Lacanian mirror in which his image was reflected, but with greater and greater diffusion. There is something unsettling about realizing that one's identity can be used as a decoy or prop, elastic in posture, eminently manipulated. The experience left me not only with severe difficulties reconciling the self/other dichotomy, but also with enough money to complete my first book of poetry, and so symptoms of self-deception persist.

Melanie Siebert, "Ditch"

Ditches are borderlands, mostly overlooked. We usually blow on by. Five million tons of road salt spread on Canadian highways every winter, unseen, toxic in high doses, seeps into the ditches and carries on downstream, but who notices? Unmown until mid-July, the ditches collect our throwaways, but also harbour species wiped out elsewhere. Places of refuse and refuge. And anyone who has had to pull over for a flat or an unplanned pit stop might recognize that sudden prickling of the senses as you find yourself not just anywhere, but somewhere, somewhere with distinctive sounds and smells and all kinds of beings going about making a life for themselves. The frayed margin between field and road. Holdout of the wild and neglected. Periphery of the known—place the poem tries to dwell.

Sue Sinclair, "Cherry Trees"

Visiting the cherry blossoms in the springtime is one of the few rituals I insist on. I've been wondering if I'm in danger of using up my quota of poems about flowering trees, but if the Japanese can do it for centuries, surely I'm allowed a decade or two.

Karen Solie, "Postscript"

This poem began in the southwest corner of Saskatchewan: the town of Eastend, south to the Montana border, and west to the Cypress Hills. Among its abandoned villages, conservation areas, archaeological and geological points of interest. It is a place of scant population rich in evidence of what—through death, desertion, the effects of time—is gone, evidence that narrates an atmosphere of absent presences. It is a place made for naturalism. I had been reading about Carl Gauss, the late-eighteenth/early-nineteenth-century mathematician and geometer whose work in non-Euclidian geometry proved crucial to ways of describing curved spaces, and whose life was encumbered with its particular sadnesses. The poem came from thinking about how sentences, metaphors, equations enact absence in their attempts to articulate presence, and vice versa. How, when a name is called, the named thing turns its real face away. The strange beauty in this: that the dimensions of what exists, what has existed, compose a wondrous presence precisely in that they're lost to us.

Nick Thran, "Aria with a Mirror and No Earplugs"

As an all-purpose bellman at the Radium Resort, one of my jobs was mopping the floor around the pool. The laundry room where housekeeping dried the towels was a quiet spot to catch one's breath. That's where I got the opening image. That image transported itself from poem to poem, finally settling in with a wonton, Waits and wailing. And only eight springs later. Phew.

Carey Toane, "Seventy-two-hour emergency"

Inspired by a City of Toronto campaign urging residents to be prepared for unexpected emergencies with seventy-two hours worth of food, water, and supplies, this poem imagines three different responses (three days, maybe, or three houses on a street) to such a crisis. It is dedicated to my husband, who spent twenty-four hours cranking the stove and playing cards with me during the January 2009 west Toronto blackout, with thanks to my *THIS Magazine* editor and friend, Stuart Ross.

Anne-Marie Turza, "Anthem for a Small Country"

Ovid said, "Believe me, one who lives well, lives unnoticed." This poem is an homage to the smallness of that good life.

Paul Tyler, "Manitoba Maples"

The saplings of this North American native sneak into being through every available pavement crack or planter pot throughout the city. At the rate they grow, Manitoba maples could canopy the city within a decade or two. As if sensing this imminent threat to civilization, dedicated tidiers of lawns patrol their fence lines, dispatching Manitoba maple sprouts, and sawing down the seed-spreading adults. Despite the efforts of such upright citizens, the tree's tenacity gives it the upper hand. Who is prey and who is predator in this epic struggle for survival? My money's on the maple. The city, it turns out, *is* a forest—Manitoba maples are a striking reminder we're only renting the space.

Patrick Warner, "The Mole"

The poem began as an exploration of the word "mole." Mole as blemish, mole as abnormal mass in the uterus, mole as atomic weight. For a while it became fixated on the image of a woman in a pair of tight moleskin pants. But it wasn't until I removed the pants altogether that the poem revealed itself to be about something more than style, something far more down to earth—tender nosed, tufted, blind, clawed, and pink.

Zachariah Wells, "To the Superb Lyrebird, that Cover Band of the Australian Bush"

Poem Notes & Commentaries

I was introduced to the Superb Lyrebird via a David Attenborough video clip posted on Facebook by poet Karen Press. I was so impressed by the critter's shameless, showy virtuosity—a quality long undervalued by Canadians—that I couldn't *not* write a poem about him. (I mean, *lyre*, come on!) I figured a sonnet combining the schemes of Petrarch and Shakespeare was a pretty good vessel for a poem about originality achieved through emulation.

Patricia Young, "Night-Running"

This poem is one in a series of poems that came out of reading the works of Havelock Ellis, a British physician and one of the most influential sexologists in the early twentieth century. To write the poems I lifted quotations from his texts and used them as launch pads. The idea that young people in eighteenth- and nineteenth-century European societies were allowed and even encouraged to *sleep* together before marriage so intrigued and surprised me, I wanted to try to imagine the emotions and details of how this would work. The poem, then, is a kind of narrative about a boy and girl who get to know each other lying side by side in her bed, with full parental approval, talking.

David Zieroth, "How Brave"

I can remember almost nothing about writing this poem, though I remember the crisis gathering before I wrote it—but the arrival of any poem creates a storm that cannot really be understood even by looking back on the time when, in my case, I was determined to articulate this view (to release it) of how to die—but that's not it either, I wasn't determined, not really: it was all easy, the little I recall—but getting to the place where the words could arrive freely, that was a struggle, a wrestling with not wanting to speak about death—well, there it is again (and why does the seriousness of the poem curiously preclude my being entirely serious here?)—a signature preoccupation in one of my favourite poems—

Jan Zwicky, "Autobiography"

Northrop Frye said: "The fact that revision is possible, that the poet makes changes not because [she or] he likes them better but because they *are* better, means that poems . . . are born not made. The poet's task is to deliver the poem in as uninjured a state as possible, and if the poem is alive, it is equally anxious to be rid of [her or] him, and screams to be cut loose from [her or] his private memories and associations, [her or] his desire for self-expression, [etc.]" ("The Archetypes of Literature," §VII of My Credo: A Symposium of Critics, *The Kenyon Review*, XII.1: 97, my italics.) I think Northrop Frye right, and it's one reason that it's a matter of justice and respect to let poems speak for themselves.

POET BIOGRAPHIES

KEN BABSTOCK is the author of three collections of poetry including *Mean*, winner of the Atlantic Poetry Prize and the Milton Acorn People's Poet Award, and *Days into Flatspin*, winner of a K.M. Hunter Award and finalist for the Winterset Prize. His poems have won Gold at the National Magazine Awards, been anthologized in Canada, the US, and Ireland, and translated into Dutch, German, Serbo-Croatian, Czech, and French. His most recent collection, *Airstream Land Yacht*, was a finalist for the Griffin Prize for Poetry, the Governor General's Literary Award and the Winterset Prize, and won the Trillium Book Award for Poetry. He lives in Toronto.

JOHN BARTON has published nine books of poetry and five chapbooks, including *Designs from the Interior, Sweet Ellipsis, Hypothesis,* and *Hymn*. A third and bilingual edition of *West of Darkness: Emily Carr, a self-portrait*, his third book, was published by BuschekBooks in 2006. Co-editor of *Seminal: The Anthology of Canada's Gay-Male Poets*, he has won three Archibald Lampman Awards, an Ottawa Book Award, a 2003 CBC Literary Award, and a 2006 National Magazine Award. He lives in Victoria where he is the editor of *The Malahat Review*.

ANNE COMPTON's most recent collection, *asking questions indoors and out* (2009), was a finalist for the Atlantic Poetry Prize. *Processional* (2005) won the Governor General's Award and the Atlantic Poetry Prize. *Opening the Island* (2002) also won the Atlantic Poetry Prize. Her critical works include *Meetings with Maritime Poets: Interviews* (2006). In 2008, Compton received the Alden Nowlan Award for Excellence in the Literary Arts.

ALLAN COOPER has published thirteen books of poems, most recently *The Alma Elegies* (Gaspereau Press, 2007). His poems have appeared in over sixty journals and anthologies in Canada and the United States. He has

Poet Biographies

twice won the Alfred Bailey Award and was a finalist for the CBC Literary Awards three times. In 1994 he received the Peter Gzowski Award. For many years he was publisher of the poetry magazine *Germination*. He continues to run Owl's Head Press from his home in Alma, New Brunswick, a small fishing village on the Bay of Fundy.

MARY DALTON is the author of five collections of poetry, the most recent of which are *Merrybegot* (Signal, 2003), *Red Ledger* (Signal, 2006), and *Between You and the Weather* (a letterpress limited edition published by Running the Goat, 2008). *Merrybegot*, winner of the E. J. Pratt Poetry Award and nominee for the Pat Lowther Award and the Winterset Award, has also been produced as an audiobook by Rattling Books. *Red Ledger*, named a Top Book of the Year in the *Globe and Mail*, was shortlisted for the Atlantic Poetry Award and the E. J. Pratt Poetry Award. Dalton lives in St. John's, where she teaches at the Memorial University of Newfoundland.

BARRY DEMPSTER is the author of sixteen books, including a novel, *The Ascension of Jesse Rapture*, a children's book, two volumes of short stories, and twelve collections of poetry. He has been nominated for the Governor General's Award twice and has won a Petra Kenney Award, a Confederation Poets' Prize, a *Prairie Fire* Poetry Contest and the Canadian Authors' Association Jack Chalmers Award for Poetry. Barry is also acquisitions editor at Brick Books. His most recent books include *Love Outlandish* (Brick), *Ivan's Birches* (Pedlar Press), and *Blue Wherever* (Signature Editions).

KILDARE DOBBS is a veteran writer and poet who was born Irish in India, brought up in Ireland, educated at Jesus College Cambridge, and who chose Canada as his country. During the Second World War he served at sea in

126

the Royal Navy, and also ashore in RN Commandos. Author of sixteen books, he won a Governor General's Award and four nominations for National Magazine Awards. His essay on Hiroshima, among others, may be found in *The Norton Reader* and other collections. In the 1960s and '70s he was a frequent broadcaster on radio and television, and he was employed as a consultant to the Canadian and Ontario Governments in the 1970s. In 2000 he was invested with the Order of Ontario. He was appointed writer-in-residence at the University of Toronto in 2002. Most of his journalism takes the form of travel writing. *Running the Rapids*, his autobiography, was published in 2005. Just published is *The Gardens of the Vatican*, with photos by his wife, Linda Kooluris Dobbs, and text by Kildare. In 1990, at the Toronto Commemoration of the Armenian Genocide, Kildare Dobbs was keynote speaker. *Casanova in Venice* is a long poem in rhyming couplets with wood engravings by Wesley Bates, which will be published in the fall of 2010 by the Porcupine's Quill.

DON DOMANSKI was born and raised on Cape Breton Island and now lives in Halifax, Nova Scotia. He has published eight books of poetry. In 2007 his book *All Our Wonder Unavenged* won the Governor General's Award for poetry and the Atlantic Poetry Prize. In 2008 *All Our Wonder Unavenged* also won the Lieutenant Governor of Nova Scotia Masterworks Arts Award. Published and reviewed internationally, his work has been translated into Czech, French, Portuguese, Arabic, and Spanish.

GLEN DOWNIE was born in Winnipeg, worked in cancer care for many years in Vancouver, and now lives in Toronto. In 1999, he served as Writer-in-Residence at the Medical Humanities Program of Dalhousie University's Faculty of Medicine. He has published fiction, nonfiction, reviews, and six books of poetry. His most recent collection is *Loyalty Management*, for which he won the 2008 Toronto Book Award.

127

Poet Biographies

SUE GOYETTE lives in Halifax and has published two books of poems and a novel. She's been nominated for several awards, including the Governor General's Award for Poetry, Pat Lowther Award, Gerald Lampert Award, and Thomas Head Raddall Fiction Award, and won the 2008 CBC Literary Prize. Her third collection of poems is forthcoming from Brick Books. Her poetry has appeared on the Toronto subway system, in wedding vows, and spray-painted on a sidewalk somewhere in St. John, New Brunswick. Sue has taught at the Banff Centre for the Arts, the Blue Heron Workshop, and the Sage Hill Experience and currently teaches in the Creative Writing Program at Dalhousie University.

ROSEMARY GRIEBEL is a Calgary poet and librarian and has been published in a variety of media, including CBC Radio, literary journals, anthologies, chapbooks, and on public buses. Her first collection of poems, *Yes*, will be published by Frontenac House in 2011.

ADRIENNE GRUBER has been shortlisted for *Arc*'s Poem of the Year contest, *Descant*'s Winston Collins Best Canadian Poem contest, and the CBC Literary Awards. She has an MFA in creative writing from UBC, and her first poetry manuscript *This Is The Nightmare* was published with Thistledown Press in September 2008. Her chapbook *Mimic* is forthcoming with Leaf Press.

JAMELLA HAGEN grew up in Hazelton, BC, and currently lives in Whitehorse. She has a Master of Fine Arts in Creative Writing from UBC and is a former executive editor of *PRISM international*. Her work has appeared in journals such as *Arc, Event, The Fiddlehead,* and *The Malahat Review*. Her first collection of poetry is forthcoming with Nightwood Editions.

STEVEN HEIGHTON's poems and stories have appeared in such magazines as

128

The London Review of Books, Poetry, Tin House, The Walrus, Europe, Agni, Poetry London, Brick, The Literary Review of Canada, Best English Stories, and *The Best Canadian Poetry in English 2009.* He has published several novels, including *Afterlands*—which appeared in six countries and was a *New York Times* Book Review editors' choice—and the recent *Every Lost Country.* He has also just published a new poetry collection, *Patient Frame.* He received the 2010 K.M. Hunter Award, in the literature category.

WARREN HEITI is a doctoral candidate and sessional instructor in philosophy at Dalhousie University in Halifax, Nova Scotia. His poetry has been anthologized in *Breathing Fire 2: Canada's New Poets* (Nightwood Editions, 2004) and *Best New Poets 2009* (Samovar Press, 2009).

M.G.R. HICKMAN-BARR, now a Canadian citizen, was born and raised in South Africa. Some of her writing reflects her love of wildlife and the wilderness as well as her deep political interests stemming from a life lived in the tribal complexities of her native Kwa-Zulu Natal. An avid traveller and an English professor, her fascination is with language—the raft for any number of immediate, unpredictable, and extraordinary journeys.

MAUREEN HYNES is a past winner of the Gerald Lampert Award and the Petra Kenney Poetry Award (London, England), and her poetry has been shortlisted for the CBC Literary Award. She has published two books of poetry, *Harm's Way* (Brick Books) and *Rough Skin* (Wolsak & Wynn), and her third collection, *Uncovered,* is forthcoming from Pedlar Press. Maureen is poetry editor for *Our Times* magazine.

MICHAEL JOHNSON is from Bella Coola, British Columbia, and lives in Vancouver. His work has appeared in *The Fiddlehead, Queen's Quarterly,*

Poet Biographies

The Malahat Review, The Southern Review, and in *The Best American Poetry* and *The Best Canadian Poetry in English 2009.* He drives a '53 Ford pick-up called "The People Eater" and manages the Vancouver Wine Vault, a cellaring company for private collectors. He is currently at work on his first poetry manuscript: *How to Be Eaten by a Lion.*

JIM JOHNSTONE obtained his MSc in Reproductive Physiology from the University of Toronto, where he is currently a doctoral candidate. He is a two-time winner of the E. J. Pratt Medal and Prize in Poetry, the recipient of a 2008 CBC Literary Award, and his work has been broadcast on CBC Radio's *Between the Covers* and published in Canadian periodicals such as *The Fiddlehead, Grain,* and *PRISM International.* Currently he edits *Misunderstandings Magazine,* a literary journal he co-founded with Ian Williams and Vicki Sloot.

SONNET L'ABBÉ is the author of two collections of poetry, *A Strange Relief* and, most recently, *Killarnoe,* both published by McClelland and Stewart. In 2000, she won the Bronwen Wallace Memorial Award for most prom-ising writer under thirty-five, and in 1999 she won *The Malahat Review* Long Poem Prize. L'Abbé has taught writing at the University of Toronto's School of Continuing Studies. She reviews poetry for the *Globe and Mail,* and is currently doing doctoral work in ecocriticism and experimental poetry at the University of British Columbia.

FIONA TINWEI LAM, a Vancouver writer born in Scotland, is the author of two books of poetry, *Intimate Distances* (finalist for the City of Vancouver Book Prize) and, most recently, *Enter the Chrysanthemum.* She is a co-edi-tor of and contributor to the nonfiction anthology, *Double Lives: Writing and Motherhood* (McGill-Queen's, 2008). Her prose and poetry have been published in over a dozen anthologies. http://fionalam.net/

The Best Canadian Poetry 2010

EVELYN LAU is a Vancouver writer who has published ten books, including the bestselling *Runaway: Diary of a Street Kid*, which was made into a CBC-TV movie. Her collections of poetry have received the Milton Acorn Award and a Governor General's nomination; her poems in literary magazines have been selected for the *The Best American Poetry* and *The Best Canadian Poetry* series, as well as winning a National Magazine Award. Her most recent volume of poetry is *Living Under Plastic* (Oolichan, 2010).

KATHERINE LAWRENCE published her first collection of poetry in 2001 with Coteau Books—*Ring Finger, Left Hand*—which won a Saskatchewan Book Award that same year. Her second book, *Lying to Our Mothers*, was published in 2006 by Coteau Books; the book was a Saskatchewan Book Award finalist. Originally from Hamilton, Katherine moved to Saskatchewan in 1982. She is a graduate of Carleton University and works as a communications and development consultant.

ROSS LECKIE is the author of three poetry books: *A Slow Light* (Signal); *The Authority of Roses* (Brick); and *Gravity's Plumb Line* (Gaspereau). He is the director of creative writing at the University of New Brunswick, editor of *The Fiddlehead*, and poetry editor for Goose Lane Editions.

TIM LILBURN has published eight books of poetry, mostly recently *Kill-site* and *Orphic Politics*. He is the author, as well, of two essay collections on poetics, *Living in the World as if It Were Home* and *Going Home*.

DAVE MARGOSHES is a Saskatchewan poet and fiction writer. His stories and poems have been widely published in magazines, anthologies, and in over a dozen books, including two volumes of poetry in the last two years: *The Horse Knows the Way* in 2009, and *Dimensions of an Orchard* in 2010.

Poet Biographies

JIM NASON's essays, stories, and poems have appeared in literary journals and anthologies in the United States and Canada. He has published two books of poetry: *If Lips Were as Red* and *The Fist of Remembering*; a third collection, *Narcissus Unfolding*, is forthcoming with Frontenac House. Jim has also published a novel, *The Housekeeping Journals*, and a short story collection, *The Girl on the Escalator* (forthcoming, Tightrope Books).

CATHERINE OWEN is the author of seven collections of poetry, the latest being *Frenzy* (Anvil Press, 2009). *Seeing Lessons* is due out from Wolsak & Wynn in 2010. A volume of essays and reviews called *Catalysts* will be released in 2011. Her work has been nominated for the BC Book Prize, the CBC Award, the Earle Birney Prize, and the Alberta Literary Award.

P.K. PAGE is the author of more than a dozen books, including poetry, a novel, short stories, essays, and books for children. Awarded a Governor General's Award for poetry (*The Metal and the Flower*) in 1954, Page was also on the shortlist for the Griffin Poetry Prize (*Planet Earth*) in 2003 and awarded the BC Lieutenant Governor's Award for Literary excellence in 2004. P.K. Page died in January 2010. Her 2009 collection, *Coal and Roses* (Porcupine's Quill), was posthumously nominated for the 2010 Griffin Poetry Prize.

REBECCA LEAH PĂPUCARU is a graduate of the Humber School for Writers (Toronto) and is currently working on her PhD in English at the University of Montreal. Her poetry and prose have been shortlisted for a number of awards in Canada, including *Arc*'s Poem of the Year Contest. In Canada, her poetry has appeared in *PRISM international* and *Existere*, and is forthcoming in *The Antigonish Review* and *Acta Victoriana*. Both her poetry and prose will be featured in an upcoming issue of *The Nashwaak Review*. In the United States, her work has appeared in *The Orange*

Coast Review, The Emerson Review, Kestrel, and *Caesura: the Journal of the Poetry Center San Jose.*

MARILYN GEAR PILLING lives in Hamilton, Ontario, and is the author of six books. Her most recent work of fiction is *The Roseate Spoonbill of Happiness* (2002) and of poetry, *The Bones of the World Begin to Show* (2009). A creative nonfiction manuscript, *Nine Days with a Stranger,* is looking for a home. Her fiction, poetry, and creative nonfiction have won prizes and appeared in most of Canada's literary magazines, and she has read her work widely, including at Shakespeare & Company in Paris, France.

BETH ROWNTREE lives in a group home in Vancouver, and if she had her way she would never stop writing.

LENORE ROWNTREE is a Vancouver painter and writer who writes every day. www.lenorerowntree.com

ARMAND GARNET RUFFO's work is strongly influenced by his Anishinaabe (Ojibway) heritage. He is the author of *At Geronimo's Grave* (Coteau Books), winner of the Archibald Lampman Award for Poetry, and the creative biography, *Grey Owl: The Mystery of Archie Belaney* (Coteau Books). In addition to poetry, he has written extensively on Aboriginal literature, publishing recently in *The Cambridge History of Canadian Literature* (Cambridge UP) and *Across Cultures/Across Borders: Canadian Aboriginal and Native American Literatures* (Broadview Press). He also recently wrote and directed a feature film adaptation of his CBC award-winning play *A Windigo Tale.* He lives in Ottawa and teaches in the Department of English at Carleton University.

LORI SAINT-MARTIN is a professor of literature at Université du Québec à

Montréal. She has published several works of academic nonfiction and two books of short stories, *Lettre imaginaire à la femme de mon amant* and *Mon père, la nuit*. With Paul Gagné, she has published French translations of some fifty works of English-Canadian fiction and nonfiction and has twice won the Governor General's Literary Award for English-French translation (2000 and 2007).

PETER SANGER has published seven collections of poetry including, most recently, *Aiken Drum* (Gaspereau Press, 2006). He is also an essayist and critic who has published several collections of prose, including *White Salt Mountain* (Gaspereau Press, 2005), *The Stone Canoe: Two Lost Mi'kmaq Texts* (Gaspereau Press, 2008), and *Through Darkling Air: the Poetry of Richard Outram* (Gaspereau Press, 2010). He has been poetry editor of *The Antigonish Review* since 1985. He lives with his wife in South Maitland, Nova Scotia.

ROBYN SARAH, born in New York to Canadian parents, has lived in Montreal since early childhood. Her poetry began appearing in literary magazines in the early 1970s, while she completed studies at McGill and the Conservatoire de musique du Québec. In 1976, she co-founded Villeneuve Publications and until 1987 co-edited its poetry chapbook series, which included first titles by August Kleinzahler, A. F. Moritz, and others. The author of several poetry collections (most recently *Pause for Breath*, 2009) and two collections of short stories, she has also published a book of essays on poetry (*Little Eurekas*) and selected poems in French translation (*Le tamis des jours*). Her poems have been anthologized in *Fifteen Canadian Poets x 2* and *x 3*, *The Bedford Introduction to Literature*, *The Norton Anthology of Poetry*, *Good Poems for Hard Times* (Garrison Keillor), *The Best Canadian Poetry in English 2009*, and elsewhere. She was recently appointed poetry editor for Cormorant Books.

134

ELEONORE SCHÖNMAIER's writing has won numerous awards including the Alfred G. Bailey Prize for best poetry manuscript, the Earle Birney Prize for Poetry, and her story "Sidereal Time" was a Sheldon Currie Fiction Award winner. She is the author of the poetry collection *Treading Fast Rivers* (McGill-Queen's University Press), which was a finalist for the Gerald Lampert Award. Recently she performed her poetry at the Music Room in Halifax, and in Rotterdam as part of the Footnote Concert Series. Her writing has been published in many magazines, including *Canadian Literature, Descant, Grain, Fiddlehead, The Antigonish Review, The New Quarterly, Arc, Event, Vallum,* and *PRISM international*. A graduate of the University of British Columbia with a Master of Fine Arts in Creative Writing, she has taught advanced fiction courses at St. Mary's University, creative writing at Mount Saint Vincent University, and has worked as a poetry mentor for the Writers' Federation of Nova Scotia.

DAVID SEYMOUR's first book, *Inter Alia* (Brick Books, 2005), was shortlisted for the Gerald Lampert Award for the best first book of poetry in Canada. His essays, poetry, and reviews continue to be published widely in literary journals. Most recently his poetry has been shortlisted for the CBC Literary Award and selected for *The Best Canadian Poetry*. David currently lives in Toronto, where he is at work on a second and third manuscript.

MELANIE SIEBERT's debut collection of poetry, *Deepwater Vee*, published by McClelland and Stewart, travels some of Canada's most threatened rivers—places both altered and untamed—and tracks their currents of myth and history. Melanie recently completed an MFA at the University of Victoria with a Social Sciences and Humanities Research Fellowship and was awarded the Lieutenant-Governor's Silver Medal. For more than ten years, she has worked as a guide on wilderness rivers across the north from Alaska to Nunavut.

SUE SINCLAIR's latest collection of poems, *Breaker*, was published by Brick Books in 2008 and was nominated for the Pat Lowther Award and the Atlantic Poetry Prize. Sue is currently studying the philosophy of beauty at the University of Toronto.

KAREN SOLIE was born in Moose Jaw and grew up in southwest Saskatchewan. Her first collection of poems, *Short Haul Engine*, won the BC Book Prize Dorothy Livesay Award and was shortlisted for the Gerald Lampert Award and the Griffin Poetry Prize. Her second, *Modern and Normal*, was shortlisted for the Trillium Prize for poetry. Her third, *Pigeon*, was shortlisted for the Pat Lowther Award, and won the 2010 Griffin Poetry Prize and 2010 Trillium Prize. She lives in Toronto.

NICK THRAN's second collection of poetry, *Earworm*, will appear in 2011 with Nightwood Editions. His first collection, *Every Inadequate Name*, was nominated for the Gerald Lampert Award. He is currently a Goldwater Teaching Fellow and MFA candidate at New York University.

CAREY TOANE is an editor, poet, and busybody currently located somewhere between Toronto and Brooklyn. She is the outgoing grants coordinator of the Scream Literary Festival, the original host of the reading series Pivot at the Press Club, and a co-founder of the mechanical journal *Toronto Poetry Vendors*. Her poems have been published in *CV2*, *THIS Magazine*, and the anthology *Dinosaur Porn* (Ferno House/The Emergency Response Unit). Her chapbook, *Ministry of the Environment*, was released in 2008 by Bench Press.

ANNE-MARIE TURZA's poems have appeared in *The Malahat Review*, *The*

New Quarterly, The Antigonish Review, Grain, and *Arc.* She lives on Vancouver Island.

PAUL TYLER's book *A Short History of Forgetting* was published in April 2010 by Gaspereau Press. His poems recently appeared in *Grain, PRISM International, The Fiddlehead* and *The Minnesota Review.* He won first place in the Being at Work Poetry Challenge, The Byron's Quill Award, and was a runner up for The Bliss Carman Award. Paul grew up on Vancouver Island and now works as a library reference assistant in Ottawa. He was on the editorial board of *Arc Poetry Magazine* from 2004–2008.

PATRICK WARNER has published three collections of poetry. His first collection, *All Manner of Misunderstanding,* was shortlisted for the Atlantic Poetry Prize in 2002. His second collection, *There, there,* published by Signal Editions (2005), was awarded the E. J. Pratt Award for poetry in 2007. His third collection, *Mole,* was published by House of Anansi Press in 2009. His poetry has been anthologized in *Coastlines: The Poetry of Atlantic Canada, Backyards of Heaven: an anthology of Newfoundland and Irish poetry, The New Canon: an anthology of Canadian Poetry,* and *The Best Canadian Poetry in English 2009.* Patrick Warner grew up in Claremorris, Co. Mayo, Ireland, but now lives in St. John's, Newfoundland.

ZACHARIAH WELLS, originally from PEI, has lived in seven provinces and territories since 1991. He is the author of numerous chapbooks and the poetry collections *Unsettled* (Insomniac Press, 2004) and *Track & Trace* (Biblioasis, 2009, shortlisted for the Atlantic Poetry Prize); the co-author, with Rachel Lebowitz, of the children's story *Anything But Hank!* (Biblioasis, 2008, illustrated by Eric Orchard); and the editor of *Jailbreaks: 99 Canadian Sonnets* (Biblioasis, 2008) and *The Essential Kenneth Leslie* (Porcupine's Quill, 2010). A prolific critic, his prose has won *Arc Poetry*

Poet Biographies

Magazine's Critic's Desk Award three times and been shortlisted for a National Magazine Award; a collection of his criticism is forthcoming from Biblioasis. Wells lives in Halifax, where he works as a passenger train attendant and as a freelance writer and editor.

PATRICIA YOUNG's tenth collection of poetry, *An Autoerotic History of Swings*, will be published in the fall of 2010 with Sono Nis Press.

DAVID ZIEROTH's most recent book of poetry, *The Fly in Autumn* (Harbour Publishing), won the Governor General's Literary Award in 2009 and was nominated for the Dorothy Livesay Poetry Prize in 2010. *Berlin Album* was published by Rubicon Press in 2009. Leaf Press will release *Hay Day Canticle* this year. He founded The Alfred Gustav Press in 2008, a micropress for publishing poetry. He lives in North Vancouver, BC. Visit www.davidzieroth.com.

JAN ZWICKY's "Autobiography" is from a forthcoming collection, *Forge*. She has published widely as a poet, philosopher, and essayist. A native of Alberta, she now lives on the West Coast.

LONGLIST OF 50 POEMS

(in alphabetical order)

1. Bachinsky, Elizabeth. "God of Panic." *ditch.*
2. Baldwin, Correy. "mrs dorothy bruce." *Arc.* 63. Winter 2010.
3. Bowering, George. "Coloured Clothes." *Event.* 37:3.
4. Chambers, Chris. "Visiting Ours." *Taddle Creek.* 13:1. The Christmas Number, 2009.
5. Christakos, Margaret. "Stuff." *The Fiddlehead.* 238. Winter 2009.
6. Conn, Jan. "Fable of Pink." *Prairie Fire.* 30:2. Summer 2009.
7. Cody, Susan. "Porridge and Ice." *Literary Review of Canada.* 17:10. December 2009.
8. deBeyer, Michael. "Untitled." *Prairie Fire.* 30:4. Winter 2009.
9. Dennis, Amy. "When There Isn't Enough Money for a Plane Ticket Home." *Descant.* 40:1. Spring 2009.
10. Donlan, John. "Strong as Life." *The Antigonish Review.* 158. Summer 2009.
11. Frank, Linda. "A Long Time Coming." *Prairie Fire.* 30:2. Summer 2009.
12. Guriel, Jason. "Three Poems." *The New Quarterly.* 109. Winter 2009.
13. Harris, Maureen Scott. "Ghazals for a Pilgrimage." *Prairie Fire.* 30:1. Spring 2009.
14. Hartsfield, Carla. "Seven, seven, oh seven." *Contemporary Verse 2.* 31:4. Spring 2009.
15. Henderson, Brian. "Unrespectable, 11 May." *Prairie Fire.* 30.1. Spring 2009.
16. Hilles, Robert. "Known." *Event* 37:3.
17. Howell, Bill. "Local Subtext." *Descant,* 40:3. Fall 2009.
18. Hutchinson, Chris. "Homeless." *The Fiddlehead.* 238. Winter 2009.

Longlist of 50 Poems

19. Joseph, Eve. "White Camelias." *The Malahat Review*. 168. Fall 2009.

20. Kidd, Monica. "Rheumatic Fever." *The Fiddlehead*. 238. Winter 2009.

21. Lane, M. Travis. "Moon Songs." *Descant*. 40:3. Fall 2009.

22. Langer, James. "Bushcraft." *Riddle Fence*. 3. Winter 2009.

23. Lemond, Edward. "Overheard." *The Antigonish Review*. 158. Summer 2009.

24. Lista, Michael. "Louis Slotan's Flaw." *Descant*. 40:3. Fall 2009.

25. Long, Angela. "English Lesson 13, The Time." *The New Quarterly*. 109. Winter 2009.

26. MacLean, Kath. "Talking, Talking." *subTerrain*. 52.

27. Martin-DeMoor, Lisa. "October." *The Fiddlehead*. 239. Spring 2009.

28. Matthews, Dale. "Lobsters." *Literary Review of Canada*. 17:10. December 2009.

29. McOrmond, Steve. "When It Comes For You." *Arc*. 63. Winter 2010.

30. Moeller, Vanessa. "The Keening of Icebergs." *The Antigonish Review*. 156. Winter 2008.

31. Mounteer, Jordan. "Sitkum Creek." *The Malahat Review*, 169. Winter 2010.

32. Munro, Jane. "Here, the air is visible." *PRISM international*. 48:1. Fall 2009.

33. Pacey, Michael. "Crowbar." *The New Quarterly*. 111. Summer 2009.

34. Pollock, James. "The Museum of Death." *The Fiddlehead*. 238. Winter 2009.

35. Porter, Pamela. "The Bandoneón Player." *Descant*. 40:4. Winter 2009.

36. Quednau, Marion. "Paradise, Later Years." *The Malahat Review*. 167. Summer 2009.

37. Rhodes, Shane. "The Positivist." *The Fiddlehead*. 238. Winter 2009.

38. Robinson, Matt. "Rotary, Roundabout." *Grain*. 36:4. 2009.

39. Rogers, Damian. "A Great Happiness Awaits." *Maisonneuve*. 32. Summer 2009.

40. Scardow, Phin. "Blind Spot." *Prairie Fire*. 30:1. Spring 2009.

41. Scheier, Jacob. "Fire Island." *Rampike*. 18:2. 2009.

42. Sparshott, Francis. "Out of Wind." *Descant*. 40:4. Winter 2009.

43. Steadman, Dean. "Crime Passionnel: A Mystery in Five Parts for (Dog) Lovers." *Descant*. 40:1. Spring 2009.

44. Stenson, Susan. "Birds of a Father." *Contemporary Verse 2*. 31:4. Spring 2009.

45. Steudel, Jeff. "Good Light." *PRISM international*. 48:1. Fall 2009.

46. Swanson, Anna. "Present Temperature." *Contemporary Verse 2*. 31:4. Spring 2009.

47. Terpstra, John. "Crossing into Heaven." *Grain*. 36:2. 2009.

48. Therrien, Richard. "Collapsing Time." *Prairie Fire*. 29:4. Winter 2009.

49. Wayman, Tom. "Wasps and the Fires." *Prairie Fire*. 30:1. Spring 2009.

50. Woods, James. "Catherine Wheel." *The Fiddlehead*. 238. Winter 2009.

MAGAZINES CONSIDERED FOR THE 2010 EDITION

The Antigonish Review
PO Box 5000
Antigonish, NS B2G 2W5
Tel: (902) 867-3962
Fax: (902) 867-5563
tar@stfx.ca
http://www.antigonishreview.com/

Arc: Canada's National Poetry Magazine
PO Box 81060
Ottawa, ON K1P 1B1
http://www.arcpoetry.ca/

Brick: A Literary Journal
Box 609, Stn. P
Toronto, ON M5S 2Y4
http://www.brickmag.com/

Canadian Literature
University of British Columbia
1866 Main Mall-E 158
Vancouver, BC V6Y 1Z1
Tel: (604) 822-2780
Fax: (604) 822-5504
can.lit@ubc.ca
http://www.canlit.ca/

Canadian Notes & Queries
PO Box 92

Emerville, ON N0R 1A0
Tel: (519) 968-2206
Fax: (519) 250-5713
info@notesandqueries.ca
http://www.notesandqueries.ca/

Contemporary Verse 2: The Canadian Journal of Poetry and Critical Writing
207-100 Arthur St.
Winnipeg, MB R3B 1H3
Tel: (204) 949-1365
Fax: (204) 942-5754
cv2@mts.net
http://www.contemporaryverse2.ca/

Dalhousie Review
Dalhousie University
Halifax, NS B3H 4R2
Tel: (902) 494-2541
Fax: (902) 494-3561
dalhousie.review@dal.ca
http://dalhousiereview.dal.ca/

dANDelion Magazine
Department of English
The University of Calgary
2500 University Dr. N.W.
Calgary, AB T2N 1N4
http://www.dandelionmag.ca/

Magazines Considered for the 2010 Edition

Descant
PO Box 314, Stn. P
Toronto, ON M5S 2S8
info@descant.ca
http://www.descant.ca/

ditch
http://ditchpoetry.com

enRoute Magazine
Spafax Canada
4200 boul. St-Laurent, Ste. 707
Montreal, QC H2W 2R2
Tel: (514) 844-2001
Fax: (514) 844-6001
http://enroute.aircanada.com/

Event
PO Box 2503
New Westminster, BC V3L 5B2
Tel: (604) 527-5293
Fax: (604) 527-5095
event@douglas.bc.ca
http://event.douglas.bc.ca/

Exile Quarterly
Exile/Excelsior Publishing Inc.
134 Eastbourne Ave.
Toronto, ON M5P 2G6
http://www.exilequarterly.com/

quarterly/

Existere: Journal of Arts and Literature
Vanier College 101E
York University
4700 Keele Street
Toronto, ON M3J 1P3
existere.journal@gmail.com
http://www.yorku.ca/existere/

The Fiddlehead
Campus House
11 Garland Court
University of New Brunswick
PO. Box 4400
Fredericton, NB E3B 5A3
Tel: (506) 453-3501
Fax: (506) 453-5069
fiddlehd@unb.ca
http://www.thefiddlehead.ca/

Filling Station
PO. Box 22135, Bankers Hall
Calgary, AB T2P 4J5
http://www.fillingstation.ca/

Geist
341 Water Street, #200
Vancouver, BC V6B 1B8

http://www.geist.com/

Grain Magazine
PO Box 67
Saskatoon, SK S7K 3K1
Tel: (306) 244-2828
Fax: (306) 244-0255
grainmag@sasktel.net
http://www.grainmagazine.ca/

The Leaf
The Brucedale Press
Box 2259
Port Elgin, ON, N0H 2C0

Literary Review of Canada
581 Markham Street, Suite 3A
Toronto, ON M6G 2L7
review@lrcreview.com
http://reviewcanada.ca

Maisonneuve Magazine
4413 Harvard Ave.
Montreal, QC H4A 2W9
(514) 482-5089
submissions@maisonneuve.org
http://www.maisonneuve.org/

The Malahat Review
University of Victoria

PO. Box 1700, Station CSC
Victoria, BC V8W 2Y2
Tel: (250) 721-8524
Fax: (250) 472-5051
malahat@uvic.ca
http://malahatreview.ca

Matrix Magazine
1400 de Maisonneuve W.
Ste. LB-658
Montreal, QC H3G 1M8
info@matrixmagazine.org
http://www.matrixmagazine.org/

The Nashwaak Review
St. Thomas University
Fredericton, NB E3B 5G3
Tel: (506) 452-0426
Fax: (506) 450-9615
tnr@stu.ca
http://w3.stu.ca/stu/about/
publications/nashwaak/nashwaak.
aspx

The New Quarterly
St. Jerome's University
290 Westmount Rd. N.
Waterloo, ON N2L 3G3
editor@tnq.ca
http://www.tnq.ca/

Magazines Considered for the 2010 Edition

Our Times
#407-15 Gervais Drive
Toronto, ON M3C 1Y8
Tel: (416) 703-7661
Toll-free: 1-800-648-6131
Fax: (416) 703-9094
office@ourtimes.ca
http://www.ourtimes.ca/index.php

Pacific Rim Review of Books
Box 8474 Main Postal Outlet
Victoria, BC V8W 3S1
Tel/Fax: (250) 385-3378
editor@prrb.ca
http://www.prrb.ca/index.html

poetry'zown
http://www.inkbottlepress.com/
POW/pow_open.htm

Prairie Fire
Prairie Fire Press, Inc.
423-100 Arthur St.
Winnipeg, MB R3B 1H3
Tel: (204) 943-9066
Fax: (204) 942-1555
prfire@mts.net
http://www.prairiefire.ca/about.
html

PRECIPICe
Department of English Language
& Literature
Brock University
500 Glenridge Ave.
St. Catharines, ON L2S 3A1
precipice@BrockU.CA
http://www.brocku.ca/precipice/

PRISM International
Creative Writing Program
University of British Columbia
Buchanan E462-1866 Main Mall
Vancouver, BC V6T 1Z1
Tel: (604) 822-2514
Fax: (604) 822-3616
http://prism.arts.ubc.ca/

Queen's Quarterly
Queen's University
144 Barrie St.
Kingston, ON K7L 3N6
Tel: (613) 533-2667
Fax: (613) 533-6822
queens.quarterly@queensu.ca
http://www.queensu.ca/quarterly

Rampike
English Department
University of Windsor

401 Sunset Ave.
Windsor, ON N9B 3P4
http://web4.uwindsor.ca/rampike

Rhythm
http://rhythmpoetrymagazine.
english.dal.ca/

Riddle Fence
PO Box 7092
St. John's, NL A1E 3Y3
(709) 739-6484
info@riddlefence.com
http://riddlefence.com/

Room
PO Box 46160, Stn. D
Vancouver, BC V6J 5G5
contactus@roommagazine.com
http://www.roommagazine.com/

Studio
http://www.ccfi.educ.ubc.ca/
publication/studio/index.html

subTERRAIN Magazine
PO Box 3008, MPO
Vancouver, BC V6B 3X5
Tel: (604) 876-8710
Fax: (604) 879-2667

subter@portal.ca
http://www.subterrain.ca/

Taddle Creek
PO Box 611, Stn. P
Toronto, ON M5S 2Y4
editor@taddlecreekmag.com
http://www.taddlecreekmag.com/

THIS Magazine
401 Richmond St. W., #396
Toronto, ON M5V 3A8
Editorial Tel: (416) 979-8400
Business Tel: (416) 979-9429
Fax: (416) 979-1143
info@thismagazine.ca
http://www.thismagazine.ca/

The Toronto Quarterly
http://thetorontoquarterly.
blogspot.com/

Vallum
PO Box 326, Westmount Stn.
Montreal, QC H3Z 2T5
Tel/Fax: (514) 237-8946
http://www.vallummag.com/

The Walrus
19 Duncan St., Ste. 101

Magazines Considered for the 2010 Edition

Toronto, ON M5H 3H1
Tel: (416) 971-5004
Fax: (416) 971-8768
info@walrusmagazine.com
http://www.walrusmagazine.com/

West Coast LINE
2027 East Annex
8888 University Drive
Simon Fraser University
Burnaby, BC V5A 1S6
Tel: (604) 291-4287
Fax: (604) 291-4622
wcl@sfu.ca
http://www.westcoastline.ca/

PERMISSION ACKNOWLEDGEMENTS

Tightrope Books gratefully acknowledges the authors and publishers for permission to reprint the following copyrighted works:

"Lee Atwater In Blowing Snow" appeared in the *Literary Review of Canada* (17.1, p. 16) copyright © 2009 by Ken Babstock. Used with permission of the author.

"Mill Creek Reverdie" appeared in the *Literary Review of Canada* (17.7, p. 16) copyright © 2009 by John Barton. Used with permission of the author.

"Heat in April" appeared in *Arc* (63, p. 30) copyright © 2010 by Anne Compton. Used with permission of the author.

"A Porcupine" and "The Toad" appeared in *Arc* (63, p. 59) copyright © 2010 by Allan Cooper. Used with permission of the author.

"Three Centos" appeared in *Riddle Fence* (4) copyright © 2009 by Mary Dalton. Used with permission of the author.

"Mary Lake Writing Retreat," from *Ivan's Birches* copyright © 2009 by Barry Dempster. Publisehd by Pedlar Press, 2009. "Mary Lake Writing Retreat" appeared in *Studio* (3.1). Used with permission of the publisher.

"It" appeared in *The Malahat Review* (169, p. 54) copyright © 2009 by Kildare Dobbs. Used with permission of the author.

"Gloria Mundi" appeared in *Prairie Fire* (29.4, pp. 16–17) copyright © 2009 by Don Domanski. Used with permission of the author.

Permission Acknowledgements

"Nocturnal Visitors" appeared in *Exile* (33.2, p. 144) copyright © 2009 by Glen Downie. Used with permission of the author.

"This Last Lamp" appeared in *enRoute* (May 2009, p. 89) copyright © 2009 by Sue Goyette. Used with permission of the author.

"Wonder" appeared in *The Malahat Review* (166, p. 30) copyright © 2009 by Rosemary Griebel. Used with permission of the author.

"The Rope" appeared in *Prairie Fire* (30.3, p. 13) copyright © 2009 by Adrienne Gruber. Used with permission of the author.

"Driving Daytona" appeared in *Event* (37.3, p. 53) copyright © 2009 by Jamella Hagen. Used with permission of the author. "Driving Daytona" is scheduled to appear in Jamella Hagen's forthcoming collection from Nightwood Editions (www.nightwoodeditions.com).

"Some Other Just Ones" from *Patient Frame* copyright © 2010 by Steven Heighton. Reproduced with permission from House of Anansi Press, Toronto. "Some Other Just Ones" appeared in *The Walrus* (March 2009, p. 59).

"The Day" appeared in *Grain* (37.1, pp. 77-78) copyright © 2009 by Warren Heiti. Used with permission of the author.

"Cattle Egret" appeared in *Prairie Fire* (29.4, pp. 56–57) copyright © 2009 by Dr. M.G.R. Hickman-Barr. Used with permission of the author.

"The Last Cigarette," from *Uncovered* copyright © 2010 by Maureen

Permission Acknowledgements

"Rupert's Land" appeared in *Grain* (37.1, pp. 19–21) copyright © 2009 by Tim Lilburn. Used with permission of the author.

"The Chicken Coop" from *The Horse Knows the Way* copyright © 2009 by Dave Margoshes. Published by BuschekBooks. "The Chicken Coop" appeared in *Queen's Quarterly* (116.1, p. 153). Reprinted with permission of the publisher.

"Black Ice" from *Narcissus Unfolding* copyright © 2010 by Jim Nason. Published by Frontenac House, 2011. "Black Ice" appeared in *The New Quarterly* (110, p. 107). Reprinted with permission of the publisher.

"White Sale" appeared in *The Dalhousie Review* (89.3, p. 306) copyright © 2009 by Catherine Owen. Used with permission of the author.

"Cullen in Old Age" from *Cullen* copyright © 2009 by P.K. Page. Published by Outlaw Editions. Reprinted with permission of the estate of P.K. Page. "Cullen in Old Age" appeared in *The Malahat Review* (167, pp. 55–58).

"Rosalind Franklin in Open-Toe Sandals" appeared in *Existere* (28.2, pp. 27–28) copyright © 2009 by Rebecca Leah Păpucaru. Used with permission of the author.

"Billy Collins Interviewed On Stage at Chautauqua" appeared in *Descant* (146, p. 135) copyright © 2009 by Marilyn Gear Pilling. Used with permission of the author.

"7 lbs. 6 oz." appeared in *Geist* (74, p. 13) copyright © 2009 by Lenore Rowntree and Beth Rowntree. Used with permission of the authors.

Permission Acknowledgements

"Aria with a Mirror and no Earplugs" from *Earworm* copyright ©
2010 by Nick Thran. Published by Nightwood Editions, 2011 (www.
nightwoodeditions.com). "Aria with a Mirror and no Earplugs" appeared
in *Event* (37.3, p. 65). Reprinted with permission of the publisher.

"Seventy-two-hour emergency" appeared in *This Magazine* (May/June
2009, p. 17) copyright © 2009 by Carey Toane. Used with permission
of the author.

"Anthem for a Small Country" appeared in *The Malahat Review* (168, p.
56) copyright © 2009 by Anne-Marie Turza. Used with permission of
the author.

"Manitoba Maples" appeared in *The Fiddlehead* (241, p. 91) copyright ©
2009 by Paul Tyler. Used with permission of the author.

"The Mole" appeared in *Canadian Notes & Queries* (76, p. 62) copyright
© 2009 by Patrick Warner. Used with permission of the author.

"To the Superb Lyrebird, that Cover Band of the Australian Bush"
appeared in *Riddle Fence* (3, p. 44) copyright © 2009 by Zachariah Wells.
Used with permission of the author.

"Night-Running" appeared in *CV2* (31.4, pp. 97–99) copyright © 2009
by Patricia Young. Used with permission of the author.

"How Brave" from *The Fly in Autumn* copyright © 2009 by David
Zieroth. Published by Harbour Publishing, 2009. "How Brave" appeared
in *The Fiddlehead* (239, pp. 64–65). Reprinted with permission of the
publisher.

The Best Canadian Poetry 2010

EDITOR BIOGRAPHIES

LORNA CROZIER has received numerous awards for her fourteen books of poetry, including the Governor General Award for *Inventing the Hawk*. She has also edited anthologies, among them *Desire in Seven Voices* and, with Patrick Lane, *Addicted: Notes from the Belly of the Beast* and two anthologies of new Canadian poets, *Breathing Fire 1* and *2*. Her most recent book is *Small Beneath the Sky: A Prairie Memoir*. She has read her work in every continent except Antarctica and last year a collection of her poems translated into Spanish was published in Mexico City. She lives in Saanich, BC, and teaches and serves as Chair in the Writing Department at the University of Victoria.

MOLLY PEACOCK is the author of six volumes of poetry, including *The Second Blush* (McClelland & Stewart, 2009) and *Cornucopia: New & Selected Poems* (W.W. Norton); a memoir *Paradise, Piece by Piece*; and a one-woman show in poems, *The Shimmering Verge*. She has been series editor of *The Best Canadian Poetry in English* since 2007, as well as a contributing editor of the *Literary Review of Canada* and a faculty mentor at the Spalding MFA Program. Her poetry, published in leading literary journals in North America and the UK, is widely anthologized, including in *The Best of the Best American Poetry* and *The Oxford Book of American Poetry*. Her latest work of nonfiction is *The Paper Garden: An Artist Begins Her Life's Work at 72* (McClelland & Stewart, 2010). She lives in Toronto.

For the Love of Poetry

www.TightropeBooks.com